Play for Sick Children

of related interest

Narrative Approaches in Play with Children
Ann Cattanach
ISBN 978 1 84310 588 6

Fun with Messy Play
Ideas and Activities for Children with Special Needs
Tracey Beckerleg
ISBN 978 1 84310 641 8

Play as Therapy
Assessment and Therapeutic Interventions
Edited by Karen Stagnitti and Rodney Cooper
Foreword by Ann Cattanach
ISBN 978 1 84310 637 1

'If You Turned into a Monster'
Transformation through Play: A Body-Centred Approach to Play Therapy
Dennis McCarthy
Foreword by Richmond Greene
ISBN 978 1 84310 529 9

Play Therapy with Abused Children
2nd edition
Ann Cattanach
ISBN 978 1 84310 587 9

Social Skills Games for Children
Deborah M. Plummer
Illustrated by Jane Serrurier
Foreword by Professor Jannet Wright
ISBN 978 1 84310 617 3

Replays
Using Play to Enhance Emotional and Behavioural Development for Children with Autism Spectrum Disorders
Karen Levine and Naomi Chedd
ISBN 978 1 84310 832 0

The Social Play Record
A Toolkit for Assessing and Developing Social Play from Infancy to Adolescence
Chris White
ISBN 978 1 84310 400 1

Play for Sick Children

Children

Play Specialists in Hospitals and Beyond

Catherine Hubbuck

Jessica Kingsley Publishers
London and Philadelphia

First published in 2009
by Jessica Kingsley Publishers
116 Pentonville Road
London N1 9JB, UK
and
400 Market Street, Suite 400
Philadelphia, PA 19106, USA

www.jkp.com

Library of Congress Cataloging in Publication Data
Hubbuck, Catherine.
Play for sick children : play specialists in hospitals and beyond / Catherine Hubbuck.
p. cm.
Includes bibliographical references and index.
ISBN 978-1-84310-654-8 (pb : alk. paper) 1. Play therapy. 2. Sick children. I. Title.
RJ505.P6.H78 2009

618.92'891653--dc22

2009001869

British Library Cataloguing in Publication Data
A CIP catalogue record for this book is available from the British Library

ISBN 978 1 84310 654 8

Printed and bound in Great Britain by
MPG Books Limited, Cornwall

Contents

Acknowledgements

Heartfelt thanks are due to the many people – friends, colleagues and family – who have given their support, encouragement and guidance in the course of producing this book.

Particular thanks are due, however, to the lovely Dom for his great patience and constant reassurance and to Sandra Dumitrescu for her support and willingness to plough through pages and pages of words. Grateful thanks also go to Suzanne Storer of the Hospital Play Staff Education Trust and Norma Jun-Tai and Judy Walker of the National Association of Hospital Play Staff for their specific guidance around a number of professional and training issues.

In addition, I would like to dedicate this book to Tara and Peter (senior!), who between them have provided the motivation for working to support sick children; to Jonathan and Peter (junior!) who have expertly alerted me to the extra special needs of babies; and also to the memory of Adi, Robert, Simon and Kieran, who with a great many other children I have met along the way, regularly serve to remind me that life is to be lived to the full.

Catherine Hubbuck (2009)

Introduction

In 1952, at the age of five, Peter was playing in a friend's house when he fell through a plate glass door. The result of this accident was a serious laceration to his lower leg and he was taken to hospital – a city Royal Infirmary about three miles away from home. Here he underwent surgery and the wound was mended, and he was discharged home fairly shortly afterwards. Within days, however, it was apparent that all was not well. The wound had become infected and required further surgery. Furthermore, the infection meant that he needed to be treated in isolation and so was moved to the local specialized Fever Hospital, where illnesses of this nature were commonly treated. He remained there for around seven weeks in an isolation room.

While, clearly, he was the only occupant of the room for this time, he was being nursed on a ward for adults, by nurses who were more accustomed to caring for adult patients rather than children. There were no toys at his disposal, though he had a train and soft panda toy brought in from home to amuse him. There was no continuation of his primary schooling, no specific play input as part of his care, little age-appropriate explanation given to him about what had happened to him and what treatment he was receiving, although he can recall being read to by one of his nurses. He had no contact during this time with anyone else, with the exception of his nurses, who were pleasant and friendly to him but did not explain why his isolation was necessary, nor offer any activity to alleviate his loneliness and boredom. For most of his seven-week stay in hospital he remained in bed, receiving daily injections of penicillin into his backside. The infected wound was regularly dressed with a dressing that was sticky and unpleasant to apply and particularly to remove.

His parents, who owned a post office, visited daily for the initial week or so of his treatment, and thereafter travelled in to see him twice a week on a Wednesday afternoon and a Sunday when the shop was closed. During these visits, because of the infection that was affecting his wounded leg, they were unable to sit with him in his room, but instead waved to their little boy through the glass door/window before returning home.

Once Peter's wounded leg had healed and the infection had cleared, he was able to return home and to resume his everyday activities. His treasured toy train and panda remained at the hospital, however, and were incinerated to prevent any further spread of infection.

In 2001, at the age of two, Tara was involved in an incident in which she was badly scalded by coming into contact with very hot water. She suffered deep burns to 32 per cent of her body and was admitted to a specialist paediatric burns unit. She was accompanied from the scene of her injury by family members. They were thereafter at liberty to remain with her throughout her stay in hospital, where trained children's nurses cared for her. Following some initial surgery, including the application of skin grafts to much of the injured area, Tara contracted the MRSA infection and had to be cared for in isolation for six weeks. During this time, she had daily contact with the hospital play specialist who brought activities to her bedside and also regularly took her for walks in the hospital grounds. She had access to toys, books and a television throughout her stay in hospital. Visiting hours on the children's unit were unrestricted and there was both bedside and limited separate family accommodation so that children could always have the company of a parent or other family member.

During her stay in hospital, Tara underwent multiple dressing changes, some under general anaesthetic and some following the administration of sedating drugs. The play specialist was present for these procedures and offered distraction through play as required. This input continued after Tara's discharge from hospital when she was seen in the unit's Outpatient department. Basic discussion and play activities were provided to prepare and acclimatize Tara to the experience of needing to wear pressure garments over her scarring for many months after her injury occurred. She was particularly taken with a large rag doll who also wore a pressure vest and glove, and would play enthusiastically with it on all her visits to the scar management teams. Through this doll and other well-planned or adapted play activities, the play specialist was able, despite Tara's young age, to help her make some sense of her hospital experiences.

In spite of the fact that Peter and Tara both experienced a similar level of injury, and subsequently succumbed to similarly unpleasant infections, necessitating a similar type of care, the differences in their experiences of being ill and in hospital are almost immeasurable. You could even say that the healthcare environments encountered by these two small children 50 years apart were worlds apart – the hospital which cared for Peter throughout his injury and the illness that followed was another world compared to that which Tara inhabited for some two months or more.

That is, of course, not to say that the nurses caring for Peter in the 1950s were any less caring or practically skilled than those who looked after Tara two generations later. The most significant difference between these two scenarios is undoubtedly the shift from, in the case of Peter, it being acceptable – normal even – for a very young child to be cared for on an adult ward for the entirety of his hospital treatment to, in Tara's case, the recognition that it is essential for children to be admitted to an area specially prepared and where staff are specifically trained to care for them. Peter's experience would, in today's health service, not only be unheard of but would stand in violation of a whole host of national and international laws, policies, recommendations and expectations.

The experiences of these two children – with their similarities and yet such striking differences – carry with them a particularly personal significance. My father, Peter, was the little boy who fell and cut his leg 56 years ago. His experience in an isolation ward was a story shared with me during my childhood. Never self-pitying, the details of that story have stayed with me ever since, influencing my decision to work with sick children, with the aim of easing them through the strains and stresses of being ill and of being made well.

Fifty years later, my own daughter Tara was admitted to hospital with a shocking burn injury. Her time spent in hospital, both in the context of today's knowledge of children's social and psychological needs as well as today's health service, serves to demonstrate the considerable changes that have been made to that experience for children and families in the time that has passed since her grandfather's hospital treatment. Their experiences have become the overarching motivation behind this book, which seeks to consider these differences, and specifically the role of the play specialists working with sick children. The development of play work in a hospital setting, the specific development of the professional role of 'play specialist' and the wider recognition of this role and work amongst others working within the wider multidisciplinary team, have almost exclusively taken place within that 50-year time period.

So then, with those two much loved children providing the motivation, this book seeks to explore the role of play specialists, especially those working in a hospital context, and in doing so to bring about an increased awareness and appreciation of their important work with sick children, young people and their families.

1

Socio-Historical Perspectives on Children and the Experience of Being in Hospital

The child in hospital, particularly when separated completely from his parents, encounters conditions similar to those of the deprived child, with the added risk of painful and frightening experiences.
(Platt 1959, p.3)

In his 1996 publication *Children in Hospital*, Richard Lansdown gives a full and informative account of the development of healthcare provision specifically for children. An outline is given of the development of children's wards within larger hospitals and charitable establishments, followed by the development of children's hospitals and staff with expertise in the care of children. Lansdown's valuable account of the little-acknowledged history of children's healthcare highlights that the specific needs of children were known and beginning to be understood by some physicians and philanthropists a long way back into history. Yet what is also apparent through this account is that the voices of those individuals who recognized the need for and made attempts at specialist provision for sick children were often unheard and certainly not widely acknowledged in social climates where children were among the very lowest ranking citizens. Lansdown acknowledges a number of these such campaigners including one George Armstrong, founder of the Dispensery for the Infant Poor in London in 1769, who is noted to have recognized even then that if a child were removed from the care of its parent (or nurse) 'you break its heart immediately' (p.6). A controversial statement indeed, especially given the social attitude to both children and the poor at that time.

Looking at the charted history of specialized children's health services, change for sick children was never going to occur on any grand scale before the status of children was raised and subsequently a priority made of preserving their state of health and wellbeing. The predominantly lone voices of those who long ago recognized and campaigned for children's health provision are particularly poignant today because the view of children is now so very different. The shift that needed to happen was for society as a whole to become receptive to the voices that were prepared to champion the cases of sick children in need of more and better support.

Should those occupied in the field of children's healthcare question why it is important to have this shift in thinking mapped out or the need to understand a little about societal changes in valuing children, perhaps their question should really involve what it is that motivates them to turn up and work every Monday morning. It is crucial to acknowledge how these key sociological shifts have had an impact on the care of children in hospital, upon children's healthcare workers and upon today's sick children themselves. Without the shift in attitudes towards children and the value placed upon them in contemporary Western society, the hospital environment now inhabited by sick children could be a dramatically different place.

No more than little adults...?

The nineteenth century was a particularly significant time through-out which the accepted view of children and childhood began to change and shift. At the beginning of this period child mortality rates were relatively high and children were not highly regarded in society by any means. The majority of children from a very young age were merely a part of the workforce of Britain, they were not often schooled apart from in a trade or skill, and moreover they were viewed and treated like little adults. There was little or no recognition for any particular children's needs or rights. If they committed an offence, they would be tried and punished as if they were an adult. If they became unwell, there was no children's provision for their needs. In fact, the notion of children's needs was rarely considered or even accepted. Through the course of the nineteenth century this view began to undergo a degree of rethinking, mainly because the needs and later the rights of children started to appear as a feature of legislation. This legislation became so far reaching that a different view of children and childhood began to emerge across the whole of society, and to lay down roots for a new approach to caring and attending to children.

These laws were first concerned with working conditions, the hours children worked and the safety (or otherwise) of the conditions in which they worked. By the later nineteenth century, greater awareness and concern for the working classes and the extreme poverty that many families lived in brought about a massive push for all children to receive some common degree of education. By the 1880s, the widescale establishment of education for all had served not only to make the notion of children working for wages somewhat unacceptable, but had also raised public awareness about the often poor physical and mental state of those school children (Hendrick, in James and Prout 1997).

Therefore, by the turn of the twentieth century not only had the status and understanding of children and childhood undergone a great change, but also recognition of their needs and of the distinction that was now made between children and adults. The education of children provided an environment in which child development and child psychology could more easily be observed and studied in a controlled manner. The emphasis at this point became much less about children's impact upon society or indeed the impact of society upon children, and much more about the development of the individual child, the significance of personal relationships, family dynamics and early experiences, and the effects of these upon behaviour or conduct.

In the best interests of the child...?

The two world wars of the early twentieth century, while profoundly changing society, potentially took some of the focus away from these studies. This was until the Second World War brought about the large-scale evacuation of children. The threat to British society was perceived as so critical as to necessitate a worldwide war effort against German fascism and the very real fear of absolute power. This brought about the largest migration of people – mainly children from urban areas – in British history. In anticipation of Britain's cities becoming easy prey for Nazi bombing raids a great many children, pregnant women and other vulnerable groups (notably such as the visually impaired) were moved from urban areas to rural homesteads. That thousands upon thousands of children could be moved from their home environments and placed into the care of total strangers seems an entirely alien concept today, in a society steeped in child protection policy, adult:child ratios and OFSTED reports. Such was a nation's fear for its self-preservation, its continuation into the generations ahead and its children's safety that this migration was deemed to be the best possible solution to the threat faced by families and the nation as a whole.

Although it may not initially appear to be linked in any significant fashion to the experiences of children in hospital, this process of moving children around the country during wartime was of great significance in understanding the effects of stress and separation of children from their parents, and in considering anew the support and assistance that was required by many families up and down the country. Hendrick (1997) suggests that the process of mass evacuation of children was significant for two main reasons. The first of these was that by uprooting children, many of whom had been living in the most urban, most deprived and most run-down of areas, evacuation 'shone a torchlight into the darkest corners of urban Britain' (p.54). Just as the Education Acts of the previous century had brought to light the deprivation of children and families, so too had evacuation highlighted that some families were still living in dreadful conditions without the possibility of helping themselves to change their circumstances.

Furthermore, the evacuation experience was highly significant in shaping theories of childcare and furthering the understanding of the importance of family relationships. For those psychologists who studied and put forward theoretical arguments about the significance of mother–child relationships and family ties, the effects of evacuation upon children and families positively confirmed their views. Once the Second World War had ended, the focus could now be reset towards the needs of families, and children in society. The lessons learned by the uprooting of many, many children, including those from some of the poorest families, and the observations of children so profoundly separated from their family bases meant that a response had to be made to the needs that had already begun to be identified.

A new state of affairs

This response largely came in the form of two major political and social milestones, the first being the 1948 Children Act. This act of parliament followed closely on from a report by the Curtis Committee, in 1946, which looked into the experiences of children in residential care. Together, these two pieces of legislation brought to the fore the crucial importance of the needs of individual children to be recognized and effectively met by those responsible for their care, and ultimately by the state. While these largely dealt with children's residential and foster care arrangements, the issues they raised were equally pertinent to children in hospital, since at this time children were cared for in separation from their parents when they were sick.

The year 1948 also heralded the birth of the Welfare State as it is known today and in particular the National Health Service, which sought to provide healthcare that was free at the point of access and no longer governed by charitable trusts or private fees. The National Health Service meant all citizens could benefit equally from treatment when they were ill and in need. In considering the impact of this upon children and families, it was no longer the case that families would have to pay for healthcare – a fact that may have led the poorest families to make tough decisions based on their financial resources, or lack thereof. Instead the responsibility fell to the state to care for those who required treatment for illness. Thus, as Hendrick (1997, p.56) suggests, the publicly cared-for child was to be treated as an individual, whose rights and needs were to be recognized and met as far as possible. Those concerned with the wellbeing of children in hospital became focused on pinpointing and addressing those needs.

In the wake of these massive milestones, the early 1950s were a time when the world was changing, particularly where the needs of children and families were concerned. The state was doing more than it had ever previously done to ensure a high quality level of health and social care was being provided for all citizens. Furthermore, a social shift was taking place that meant children – having previously been seen as resilient enough to withstand being uprooted and placed into the care of strangers – were now accepted as desperately in need of the continuous care of their main, safe carer, usually their mother, whether that care was given day-to-day at home or in the strange and stressful environment of the hospital. That shift in itself is immeasurable and significant. It spells a starting point for understanding more wholly and more sensitively the needs of children and the potential effects on a child's mental health – short and long term – of having that relationship somehow interrupted or threatened.

James and Joyce Robertson

In the light of this shift and at around the same time that Peter, the little boy featured in our introduction, was unwell, somewhere in another UK hospital, James and Joyce Robertson, psychologists based at the Tavistock clinic and Tavistock Institutes of Human Relations, were studying what hospital was like for children. Their work, which began in 1948, was concerned with looking into the reactions of children when separated from their mothers in various care settings. In their ground-breaking film entitled *A Two-Year-Old Goes to Hospital*, the Robertsons mapped out in stages the experiences of a little girl admitted to hospital for eight days to have an umbilical hernia repaired and graphically showed her reactions to this experience.

A significant influence on this study was the work of John Bowlby whose theory and discussion around maternal deprivation was ground-breaking then and, despite a certain degree of challenge (notably by Michael Rutter in 1972), remains significant today. Bowlby's work on attachment focused particularly on the relationship between mother and child and put forward the theory that the foundation of good adult mental health and relationships was a warm, loving and mutually satisfying bond between a child and his or her mother. In stating this, Bowlby also made the point that optimal bonding between a mother and child required more than simply love. Moreover, what this relationship – which gives a child his or her sense of security – relies upon is an attentive responsiveness to the cues sent out by a baby or young child in communication of his or her needs. This attunement is of great value to the depth and strength of the mother–child bond. (Later this view was challenged by Rutter, who postulated that relationships with other close family members, especially fathers, were also as crucial and meaningful as that with the child's mother.)

At its core, the Robertsons' study stated that during their earliest years, children are dependent upon the maintenance of a safe and protected relationship with their parents, particularly their mother, because they are the people who make their world stable and secure (Robertson 1970). The Robertsons therefore wanted to address what the experience was like for children if they were admitted to hospital during this critical stage of development – that is from birth to around the age of five. With their extensive knowledge of children's development and the significance of familial relationships, the Robertsons presented a case that was disturbing and sobering to health professionals at the time and which called for some effective changes to be made for children requiring hospitalization.

It was their claim that when a young child has a deeply loving and trusting relationship with his or her parents – themselves the embodiment of all that is safe and reliable – and must encounter a strange and clinical environment such as that presented by the hospital without their constant presence, the child will experience such an extreme failure of love and security that he or she will be overwhelmed and potentially devastated by the experience. The Robertsons' presentation showing a child's emotional reaction to being without her mother – her secure base – at the time when she most needed to be in her reassuring presence was so direct as to be unequivocal in demonstrating the need for major changes to be made in how young children were cared for in hospital.

The work of the Robertsons was significant because it identified three stages that children go through during the separation and stress caused by hospitalization, namely protest, despair and detachment. They also put forward the two most significant dangers of hospitalization for young children as being the potential for them to experience 'the traumatic', where the shock of 'losing' their mother coupled with the stress of having to endure unpleasant invasive procedures may be more than they can tolerate, and also 'the deprivational', which involves long-term separation from their mother and maternal-type care and could lead to 'serious impoverishment of the personality' (Robertson 1970, p.20).

The Platt Report, 1959

By way of a response to the growing awareness of children's needs when they were sick and required hospital treatment, a committee was established by the Central Health Services Council – part of the Ministry of Health – to find out about, discuss and ultimately make recommendations regarding the welfare of children in hospital. This group was chaired by Sir Harry Platt, a distinguished surgeon of the day, and in 1959 a document containing these observations, findings and recommendations of the committee was accepted by the ministry (Platt 1959).

The Platt Report – as it has widely become known – was received favourably by healthcare professionals and lay-people alike, making many significant statements on the effects of hospitalization on children and their families, while suggesting many sensitive and intelligent, practical and theoretical solutions to the difficulties most often encountered. Three of the recommendations for change contained within the Platt Report that commanded considerable attention were:

- that visiting to children should be unrestricted

- that provision should be made to enable mothers – particularly those with children under five years old – to stay with their children in hospital

- that the training of medical and nursing students should be improved by the inclusion of information to give a greater understanding of the emotional needs of children.

While the Ministry of Health adopted recommendations in the Platt Report as official policy, such a policy could not be enforced because it was not possible to produce legislation based solely on professional judgements such as those contained within the report (Robertson 1970). Therefore, while it was suggested to all hospitals caring for children that the recommendations be implemented, there was no way that they could be enforced. As a result a ground-breaking project and report was relatively unable to deliver much of the change and promise suggested by its contents, and progress based on its recommendations was slow. While the Platt Report effectively and coherently demonstrated the inappropriateness of many established practices, it took time to shift from traditional beliefs about children and the old methods of caring for them to a more acceptable way of practising. In spite of this, the overriding legacy of the Platt Report is that it breathed a freshness and new motivation into a trend that was moving towards big changes.

The observations made by the committee in the mid-1950s of the needs of children and young people in hospital can be accepted as still being relevant to the experiences of sick children today. That Platt's recommendations were not able to be made legislation and therefore saw an undesirably slow – though steady – response is still frustrating. In considering the report's significance for play specialists today, however, it must be acknowledged that this is the document in which the benefits of play and recreational activities for sick children were first given explicit recognition. The Platt Report will remain significant in the professional history of hospital play staff because it marks a crucial point in time when the seeds of a specific role for play workers in hospital were sown.

The establishment of NAWCH and involvement of Save the Children

In the wake of the Platt Report, slow and steady change began to take place in hospitals throughout the UK during the 1960s. Over several years, restrictions on visiting children in hospital gradually became relaxed and by gaining this freer access to their sick children, parents realized that there was a real need for them to have the opportunity to play in hospital as they would while at home (Hales-Tooke 1973). Therefore, hospital wards became compelled to consider arranging more organized play activities for the children in their care. Support for such play schemes was provided in part by the National Association for the Welfare of Children in Hospital (NAWCH), an organization originally founded by four mothers in 1963 and set up to campaign for better provision for the needs of children and families in hospital. NAWCH and the Pre-school Playgroups Alliance began establishing more organized play activities for children in hospital settings in 1967, initially run by a workforce of volunteers and later on a more professional basis with a salaried play worker. These were not, however, the first hospital play schemes to be established. At the tail end of the 1950s and before, the observations and recommendations of Harry Platt and his committee had either been shared or heeded by a number of proactive and suitably influential professionals – including paediatricians and play experts – who had been able to establish a handful of hospital play schemes. Equally, the charity Save the Children was responsible for setting up play projects in areas where 'deprived children' and families made up much of the population. In 1962, Susan Harvey, part of the Save the Children playgroup team, put forward the suggestion that the hospital environment presented as one in which children were deprived of their usual play activities and as a result the first hospital playgroup was started at the Brook Hospital in Woolwich, in 1963. Aside from these examples, the work of NAWCH – which became Action for Sick Children in 1990 – was significant as it heralded the beginnings of the hospital play provision that is now commonplace and the professional staffing that is accepted as essential in today's paediatric healthcare settings.

As the organization of play provision for children in hospital gathered momentum, there was an increased recognition of the value of the role of hospital play workers for sick children and families. There was also a growing acceptance of the need for them to receive training and consequently to be employed as members of the ward staff rather than working on a purely voluntary basis.

Training play 'specialists'

'Hospital Play Specialist' was a title originally coined in the 1970s in recognition of the work of a group of professionals who used play with children in hospital, but were neither play therapists nor simply playleaders (NAHPS website). The creation of this title was borne out of the establishment of the first training course for those providing play in a hospital setting. This course was run at London's Chiswick College, and its first external examiner was Dr Hugh Jolly, a key exponent of the need for children to have adequate access to play in hospital.

Over that 35-year period, the training itself has become recognized more widely in professional terms, notably by becoming the nationally recognized qualification for hospital play specialists in 1992, by being jointly validated by BTEC/Edexcel from 1995, and by its accreditation to a level four award on the National Qualification Framework in 2004 (HPSET website). In the UK at the current time, therefore, the qualification required for registration and ideally – but not automatically – for employment as a play specialist is a Professional Diploma in Specialized Play for Sick Children and Young People.

The minimum entry requirements to being accepted on this training course are a professional childcare qualification at level three (on the National Qualification Framework) or above, plus at least three years post-qualifying experience in direct work with children. Some will come to the training having studied – often to quite a high level – in areas such as psychology, sociology, teaching, nursing or childhood studies. Therefore the majority of play specialists have wide-ranging experience of working with children in a variety of childcare settings prior to undertaking their specialized play training.

While undertaking their training, student play specialists must either be employed as play specialist or play assistant in a hospital, hospice or neonatal unit, or otherwise must complete a lengthy placement in a hospital play environment, under the supervision of a registered play specialist. He or she must demonstrate a high level of skill in the observation of children, the consideration of how best to communicate and adapt working methods and in the reflection on their own practice as well as that of others. They must visit, compare and contrast a range of hospital wards and healthcare settings, consider the types of specific situations faced by sick children and their families and investigate the kinds of resources that may be used to enable them to cope as well as possible with those experiences. Play specialist students must also undertake an investigative piece of research, which considers the role of the play specialist in a given setting or scenario. Once students have successfully completed the programme of study and signed the Code of Conduct they are entered onto the register held by the Hospital Play Staff Education Trust (HPSET). Periodically this registration with HPSET must be renewed and evidence of the individual's professional development maintained in a portfolio which may be called on for audit and professional monitoring. This record of professional development demonstrates the competency of play specialists in their training, knowledge and practice.

The resulting outcome of the broad mix of people who undertake this training is a strong professional body of individuals with diverse backgrounds and skills, but an overriding shared motivation to positively enhance and support the lives of sick children and young people. Play specialists therefore represent a skilled and able work-force. Yet while the profession incorporates a much-varied mixture of people with wide-ranging styles of working, what is remarkable is the breadth of input that play specialists are increasingly having in the lives of young hospital patients and within many healthcare settings, departments and teams – a change that has occurred in a relatively short space of time.

Setting professional standards for hospital play services

In 1989 the Save the Children Fund (SCF) commissioned an investigative piece of work, entitled *Hospitals: A Deprived Environment for Children? The Case for Hospital Play Schemes*. This document was specifically concerned with documenting the progress of hospital play schemes since their establishment by Susan Harvey (with the Save the Children Fund) in 1963. Furthermore it also considered the state of play provision for children within hospital environments at that time and found that despite slow, gradual yet positive progress in the establishment of play activities and services in a range of paediatric settings, there was still much to be done to create an environment where children's emotional and psycho-social needs were genuinely recognized and given an appropriate level of response.

This investigation came on the back of a survey conducted four years earlier in 1985 by the partnership of the Save the Children Fund and the Play in Hospital Liaison Committee which clearly highlighted that while those working with children appreciated the importance of play, managers and healthcare planners did not give it any high priority (Hogg 1990). These two documents led to an audit or benchmarking tool, *Quality Management for Children: Play in Hospital* – which was produced by Christine Hogg for the Play in Hospital Liaison Committee. This proved to be a highly significant document that allowed play specialists and others concerned with the provision of good quality play facilities for sick children to monitor and evaluate their service. By outlining a set of standards for hospital play services and equipping play specialists to evaluate their work, they could also more confidently appeal for greater support – personal, professional and financial – from those who held the purse strings as well as those whose aim it was to create the vision of better health services for sick children and their families.

In the same year as Christine Hogg produced this relatively ground-breaking document, NAWCH (1990) released a comparable tool – also edited by Christine Hogg with June Jolly – for the similar purpose of setting standards for adolescents in hospital and for monitoring the effectiveness and acceptability of services for teenage patients throughout the UK.

The National Service Framework for Children

Nearly two decades have passed since the Save the Children Fund and the Play in Hospital Liaison Committee sought both to investigate and provide the tools to raise the profile of play services for sick children. Children's services throughout the UK have, in that time, been forced to undergo some significant changes. This is partly due to the change of government that has taken place, but is also in response to some significant events involving children in receipt of state medical care. Of particular significance, for example, are the deaths of children undergoing heart surgery at Bristol Royal Infirmary between the mid-1980s and mid-1990s and the case of Victoria Climbié, who had become known to both health and social work professionals in the weeks and months leading up to her tragic death in 2002. These cases have rather forced the need for change as outlined in the concerns and recommendations of the Kennedy (2001) and Laming (2003) reports that followed these examples respectively.

The response to these changing times and these particular incidents is the National Service Framework for Children, Young People and Maternity Services (NSF). This document, first introduced in 2003, sets standards for children throughout the health and social care services on offer to them from pre-birth (hence the inclusion of maternity services) to their nineteenth birthday (Department of Health 2003). It is of particular significance to those involved in the provision of play for sick children since it serves to promote hospital services that are child- and family-centred and because it makes specific reference to the role and the importance of the play specialist involved in the care of children in hospital. Significantly, the NSF does more than simply acknowledge that children benefit from play provision or that play specialists are merely a part of the wider multidisciplinary team. This document states that play provision in a hospital context can have a therapeutic value, is proven to hasten recovery, and crucially recommends that children staying in hospital should have daily access to a play specialist. This is a great step forward for play specialists working with sick children today and suggests that the NSF may well be the linchpin in bringing about an increase in financing and resourcing more play specialist posts, and will act to promote and encourage support throughout the multidisciplinary team of the role of the play specialists at work with sick children.

Interestingly, this document appears to re-promote quite a number of the issues first raised 55 years before in the Platt Report, reiterating the need for children to be cared for in specialized paediatric ward settings, that parents should usually be considered the experts on their children and should accompany them throughout their stay in hospital and that children should be given an appropriate and adequate amount of information to enable them to cope with the experience of being in hospital. In addition, the NSF – created in the wake of the Victoria Climbié Inquiry – emphasizes the need to safeguard children's welfare and safety and also focuses on working in partnership with children, young people and their parents as active participants in the care they receive.

To assist play specialists to monitor and evaluate the play provision on offer to sick children and young people in hospital – particularly in the light of the new discussions and recommendations regarding play made within the NSF – a successor to Christine Hogg's 1990 audit tool was produced by Judy Walker in 2006. This document – entitled *Play for Health: Delivering and Auditing Quality in Hospital Play Services* – acknowledges and promotes the ways that the play specialist's role has evolved and developed since 1990 and provides a renewed set of standards for hospital play provision throughout today's health service. Within the introduction to this document, Walker celebrates the notion of making progress stating that this is something of a professional obligation (Walker 2006). It is heartening to find this echoing the personal hope of Harry Platt who, in 1959, expressed the desire that the results of his own enquiry would consolidate the progress and advance of the new concept of childcare newly under way in the hospitals of the day.

To return, then, to the experiences of the two children we met in the introduction, it is clear that in the time between Peter's injury and that endured by his granddaughter, Tara, a great many changes have altered almost every aspect of children's healthcare provision. Being mindful of all the contributory factors outlined above, there are four significant differences that can be observed between the two contrasting experiences:

- the expectation that parents will be fully present and involved in the care of their sick child and the provision of facilities in support of this

- specialized paediatric settings with specially trained paediatric staff

- an increased awareness across the multidisciplinary team of the psychological and emotional needs as well as physical wellbeing of patients

- full access to play and recreational activities for children, provided by trained professionals, across a wide variety of healthcare settings.

Great concerns and important research into the care and treatment of sick children have informed much government discussion and public concern in the past half-century. The result has been a lot of work that has highlighted the many needs of sick children and young people and their families. Response to these needs has included the setting up of charities such as Action for Sick Children and significant developments in the training of specialized professionals to work with children in hospital and other health-related settings, hospital play specialists being a very good example of this. The aspect that remains the same, however, despite any passage of time and continues into the future is the potential for children to be affected by the experience of being unwell and undergoing treatment for their condition.

Some of the most influential observations of children in hospital, such as those made by James and Joyce Robertson, by Harry Platt and his committee, by Susan Harvey and her colleagues at the first hospital play schemes, were made many years ago, in contexts that are now greatly altered. These observations and indeed the observers themselves contributed to a great many changes taking place in children's healthcare services. In the intervening years, there has been relatively little written specifically about play provision for sick children, although some high quality journal articles plus two notable audit tools have been produced and have contributed to the steady growth in recognition for the play specialists' work. Even so, it should be accepted that the relatively aged books and articles that are referred to throughout this book concerned with issues faced by sick children, young people, families and hospital teams are still useful and can continue to represent a relevant voice.

Furthermore, there is a significance and a relevance that is retained because they depict starkly and simply the experiences of children at a point in their lives when they need the adults from whom they are receiving care to respond sensitively and appropriately to their needs. While the environments and professionals involved in children's healthcare may have undergone dramatic changes, the experiences of children themselves do not, nor do the potential reactions to their circumstances. Susan Harvey and Anne Hales-Tooke's observation (1972) that going into hospital may be the first major crisis in a child's life or Hugh Jolly's statement (1976) that play in hospital makes tolerable the new and strange things that happen in that environment, are as true and as relevant in the course of developing an understanding of the needs of sick children today as they were 30 or 40 years ago.

This book therefore aims to provide a bridge between the old, valued thinking about the needs of sick children and a new exploration of the scope – the breadth and depth – of the role of the play specialist. Here the why and how of the play specialist's work will be explored and a picture built up of the different facets of a multifaceted role will, it is hoped, emerge. In considering what being unwell and receiving treatment is like for children – particularly based in a hospital setting – this book will explore how ably the play specialist can identify a child's individual needs and how skilfully he or she can respond to those needs. It will seek to provide a sense of affirmation for play specialists themselves in their valuable work with sick children and young people while informing other professionals about the role and importance of play in alleviating the chaos and confusion that illness, treatment and recovery can bring to the sick child and his or her family.

2

What Play Specialists Do – and What They Don't

An unoccupied child [in hospital] is less likely to be happy than one with interesting things to do. Where play can be organized under skilled supervision it is particularly useful. (Platt 1959, p.25)

What is a play specialist?

Play specialists are children's practitioners who have undertaken specialized training in the provision of play for sick children and young people largely within a hospital setting. In his 1976 article in *The Times*, appealing for more play services for sick children, Hugh Jolly states that it is by an understanding of child development and hospital work that 'the play specialist helps the child to cope with the experience of being in hospital' (Jolly 1976). While the health service and training have inevitably evolved and somewhat shifted shape, Jolly's statement still succinctly, yet accurately, serves to describe the role of the play specialist today. The training outlined in the first chapter of this book, which began some 35 years ago, continues largely to follow a similar form. Therefore, armed with a sound knowledge of child development and the value of play for all areas of that development, individuals come to learn more about why and how to provide play for children in a variety of hospital wards and other healthcare settings.

The changing work of the play specialist

It is not so long ago that a significant majority of 'play specialists' were individuals who could be found working specifically with sick children and young people within the children's ward of a hospital, providing a range of normalizing play activities, and based largely within the ward playroom. Some of these play staff were specifically trained in hospital play work, others had undertaken training as nursery nurses, others still were untrained – although with experience of working with children – and some worked on a voluntary basis.

We live in changing times. Within the health service generally, provision for sick children and young people, including the breadth of hospital play services now offered, is currently witness to some major changes. Methods of play work, its delivery and the environments wherein this work is carried out, are constantly evolving and being remodelled to meet the needs of children and to improve the service of the teams widely involved in patient care.

It is still the case that the majority of individuals who have undertaken specific training in the provision of play for sick children and young people are found working within hospital settings and are therefore known as 'hospital play specialists'. The scope for the role of the play specialist and the work they offer, however, is increasingly becoming wider, more varied and potentially increasingly specialized. Recognition not only of the needs of children within a variety of healthcare settings, but also of the impact that good quality play provision can have for those children and young people by service providers and managers is steadily increasing. As a result, the call for more play specialists has gained in volume and enthusiasm over time and the variety of work provided by hospital play staff gradually, but with a sense of certainty, increases accordingly.

The direct result of this sure and steady progress is that play specialists are now not only found within the ward playrooms, but throughout the hospital environment. They are based on a wide range of paediatric ward settings, providing play services in designated play areas, at bedsides and in treatment rooms. They work in outlying areas such as Outpatients, Accident and Emergency and X-ray departments. They work at the frontline of care, accompanying children to operating theatres, or throughout clinical procedures and treatment regimes including radiotherapy, for example. They work in isolation wards with children undergoing bone marrow transplant or treatment for serious infectious diseases and they support the sickest children being cared for within paediatric intensive care units.

Furthermore, as more children receive a greater amount of care in their own homes from community-based teams, the number of community play specialists is rising, as is that of those who practise within large healthcare centres, working alongside health visitors, general practitioners and nurses there.

Charitable health services similarly often show a clear understanding of the value of holistic care that includes play for sick children. Play specialists working within children's hospices are often important members of teams that care for life-limited children and those expected to die in childhood, with a central involvement in providing valuable support for families – parents, siblings and the sick children themselves. They contribute to both the respite and end-stage care that children receive. Play specialists may also be a part of bereavement support teams, and patient support groups, either as part of their hospital, community- or hospice-based role, or in an independent capacity.

Such is the professional knowledge and practical ability of play specialists, that they are gradually becoming more involved in taking on an increasingly central role within the planning and delivery of care for sick children in the variety of settings previously outlined, as well as undoubtedly in others, too.

The paradox within hospital play services

As the scope of the work taken on by play specialists becomes broader, the value placed on the work they deliver increases, at least at a local hospital trust or individual practitioner level. In spite of this, however, there remains something of a paradox, which is that, as a professional group, it is still quite common for play specialists to experience a sense of struggle in gaining an appropriate level of recognition for their work and their role within a wider team, and also to gain opportunities to profile the extent to which their practice benefits the children and young people with whom they work. The steady progress of the profession here outlined has been and continues to be the result of a great many play specialists (and some supportive, often influential and well-placed colleagues) tirelessly working for the greater benefit of children in hospital, and their children and future generations of children still to come by the provision of good play services. As an understanding of the play specialist's work gradually deepens, there is continually a need to keep raising the profile of play in hospital and the benefits to children and young people receiving their services.

The lack of recognition for play specialists could be for a number of different reasons. First, the play sector generally is now only just being given due recognition whereas the areas of youthwork and education have, over decades, a more professional history. Second, play roles in healthcare setting are very much in the minority compared to nursing, medical, allied health professional and hospitality roles. The result is often that play specialists do not seem to have gained a wider recognition to the same extent as other professional groups. Third, a wider understanding and acknowledgment of the work of play specialists could be compromised somewhat because their practice does not adhere to nationally centralized or recognized procedures, routines or a standardized method of work that can more readily be found in other sectors.

The extent to which there is a recognizable structure adopted for working varies significantly between teams. Play specialists may work individually or in teams and generally adapt their practice to the environment in which they are based and the people with whom they work. The beauty of this somewhat 'free-form' sense of working is that it can allow a freedom to practise according to the immediate needs of individual children or a specific working environment. A downside of this freedom, however, is that it definitely has the potential also to contribute to a lack of clarity within healthcare teams or the wider public over what play specialists do in their work. If this lack of clarity is experienced by those working relatively closely with play specialists in a multidisciplinary care team, for example, it may result in full advantage of play services offered not being taken up.

Furthermore, and perhaps somewhat controversially, it may even be suggested that in some circumstances play specialists themselves require greater clarity regarding their role and scope of work, such is the variation in the environments and styles of working from hospital to hospital, or between other healthcare settings. This could certainly be the case for those coming into the profession anew, but arguably a re-evaluation may also be beneficial to those already practising, yet who are learning how to adapt their practice within today's ever-changing health services and for whom a lack of direction or clear boundaries of work could result in practice that is somewhat limited and which does not adequately promote the beneficial effects of good quality play services for sick children. This is particularly pertinent given the relatively rapid changes in the breadth and understanding of the play specialist's role in recent years, in addition to the likely changes ahead in how they train and gain experience. These elements, amongst others, have the potential to further complicate the understanding of the play specialist's role in working with sick children and young people and therefore require play staff themselves to adopt a sense of confidence and certainty in their own practice.

In order for play specialists to promote their work and, by example, show the difference that can be made to sick children and young people through that work, there is a need to have a clear understanding of what play specialists are, what they do, those things they are not, the professional lines that are drawn by which their practice is restricted and the areas where these lines are somewhat blurred. What follows, therefore, is an overview of the role and identity of play specialists – particularly those whose work is based in a hospital setting. Within this it is also worth considering those roles that appear or sound as though they are similar to that of a play specialist or with which their role is commonly confused. By understanding the differences between such roles it is hoped that a better understanding will also be gained not only of the work of play specialists but also of certain other practitioners who work alongside them to enhance and improve the lives and experiences of children within health services.

Play specialists are not play therapists

The British Association of Play Therapists (BAPT) – one of two professional bodies with whom practising play therapists can register – define play therapy as being an effective therapy that helps children modify their behaviours, clarify their self-concept and build healthy relationships. Through play therapy, a child can enter into a dynamic relationship with the therapist that enables him or her to express, explore and make sense of difficult or painful experiences (BAPT website). Play therapists work with children, often over an extended period of time, allowing them to play freely, often with little or no adult guidance or intervention (this is known as non-directive play therapy). The play therapist observes the choice of game, plaything or the themes that the child chooses to explore or to which he or she may repeatedly return. Over the period of involvement, a play therapist aims to increase the child's insight into him- or herself, to decrease internal conflict and to encourage resiliency and coping by gently reflecting their observations to the child. It is an aim of play therapy that this process allows exploration and change to take place gradually and naturally within the child.

The children typically referred to a play therapy service might include those who are suffering from a range of psychological difficulties, such as depression, anxiety, aggression, learning difficulties or Attention Deficit Hyperactivity Disorder (ADHD), or those who have experienced complex life experiences, which may include abuse, grief, family breakdown, domestic violence or trauma. While some of the children play specialists may encounter within a healthcare setting might have experienced these types of difficulties, it is not the role of the play specialist to attempt the complex work of a play therapist. Play therapy is a distinct intervention that should only be entered into by the specifically trained professional, in receipt of an appropriate referral.

Cattanach (2003) suggests that aside from different training, styles of working and goals, a feature that differentiates play therapy specifically from the work of the play specialist is also the use of contracts drawn up between the referring care team, play therapist, the child and his or her family. These contracts outline specifically the work that is to be undertaken by the child and therapist together, the boundaries of such work and the outcomes expected or hoped for. Contracts of this nature do not tend to be used within the work of the play specialist, although the written planning, observations and the recording of outcomes is definitely encouraged.

One difficulty faced regularly by play specialists is that colleagues or patients and their families often mistakenly refer them to as 'the play therapist'. This is usually a simple mistake, although it may pose a problem for play specialists if there is an expectation that a more psychological approach and therapeutic process of working will be provided for patients. A key approach towards attempting to change this common mistake is to simply and politely, but persistently, correct those who refer to play specialists as 'therapists'. Alongside this, aiming to make the role of the play specialist as clearly understood as possible by educating colleagues on the role of play specialists is also important. By taking the opportunity to discuss their work with colleagues during everyday planning or problem solving and while also aiming to contribute to any in-house, informal training on offer to a variety of healthcare professionals, play specialists gain a valuable opportunity to raise awareness of the scope of their work and the need for therapeutic play – as opposed to play therapy (see section below) – for sick children.

Therapeutic play vs. play therapy

Because of the confusion posed by similar but ambiguous job titles and levels of professional training, and the baseline difficulty encountered by some play specialists in simply gaining recognition for the work they do, there is commonly a degree of misunderstanding in distinguishing between the terms 'play therapy' and 'therapeutic play'.

It is perhaps worth considering, at this point, that under the right circumstances virtually any positive activity can have a therapeutic outcome for someone by whom it is undertaken. A brisk walk, chatting with friends or reading a good book could all be described as being 'therapeutic' to someone who experiences a positive outcome after doing any or all of these things. Therefore a key distinction can be made between something being 'therapeutic' and it being recognized as a 'therapy'. These could perhaps be accepted as being the *process* and the *purpose* of the activity experienced by an individual. While the approach of play specialists and play therapists may at times be similar, and the work of both professionals can significantly benefit the children receiving their care, the purpose of their work is different, as is the process through which those beneficial outcomes are achieved.

Play therapy as previously discussed is a distinct and recognized therapeutic process which uses play as its means of facilitating work between therapist and client. This work is distinct from hospital play and other types of play provided for sick children because these two types of play work, so often confused with one another, have very different and distinctive purposes to them. Play therapy is the space within which a child can gain insight and skills necessary for greater emotional resilience and coping.

While a less psychologically based or analytical process, play in hospital constitutes the provision of play that can be therapeutic for children in its purpose to bridge the gap between the respective normal and abnormal environments of home and hospital. The provision of specialized play for sick children – or therapeutic play – delivered by specially trained play staff facilitates relaxation and the expression or exploration of complex emotions, and helps to build trust and better communication with those around them. As these outcomes of the play specialist's work with sick children and young people are beneficial and of positive worth in many ways, such play provision must be recognized as being therapeutic in its own right.

While being distinct from play therapy for children, the therapeutic value of play provision of the play specialist deserves recognition and validity. Gaining such recognition can be a challenge within a profession that is not widely understood and commonly referred to as play therapy.

Play specialists are not psychologists

Psychologists are individuals who have baseline training in psychology. Clinical psychologists are professionals who use that baseline training to work with clients in a clinical setting such as hospitals or within community mental health teams. It is their aim to reduce psychological distress and to enhance and promote psychological wellbeing (Batmanghelidjh 2006).

In a hospital or similar healthcare setting, psychologists are often based or assigned to work on children's wards where they may be requested by referral to work with children, parents, possibly siblings, and also with staff.

Of the professions and roles contrasted with that of play specialists in this book, the role and work of a psychologist can be seen to include a degree of similarity in nature. Play specialists often engage in conversations or activities with sick children and young people that touch on difficult subjects in order to ease anxiety, clarify confusion and bring about a greater level of understanding. That is to say, they either deal with things that are difficult to talk about (emotional or physical reactions to illness or treatment, for example), difficult to understand (such as complicated treatment) or difficult to cope with (including fears or phobias). A psychologist's involvement with children and families may also explore issues of this type, although a psychologist is likely to work on these difficult areas in a greater degree of detail or by basing his or her practice on a particular school of psychological or theoretical thought, such as cognitive behavioural therapy.

Play specialists use planning and distraction through play to assist children in their coping with painful, lengthy or distressing procedures. Psychologists may also introduce a range of coping strategies to encourage or facilitate better coping particularly during stressful hospital experiences, although they might employ a more theoretical approach or technique, such as Guided Imagery. Sometimes play specialists and psychologists will work directly alongside each other with children and families, especially if they are discussing or preparing them for complicated treatment or a serious operation such as a transplant or oncology treatment.

Regardless of the level of involvement with patients that might be shared between the psychologist and play specialist, it is important to have an understanding of where the professional boundaries lie so that play specialists can work effectively with children but also know when it is appropriate to refer patients to a psychologist if a greater level of help or involvement is required. Play specialists attempting to deliver support at a level more appropriate to that of a psychologist are in a dangerous position of overstepping those professional boundaries, which can have an impact on the play specialist, the children with whom he or she is working and future work within the multidisciplinary team.

Play specialists are not (yet) allied health professionals

At this point in time, the role of the play specialist in the UK is not currently included in the group known as allied health professions. 'Allied health professions' is the group name given to a range of specialist roles that are recognized as being vital to the provision of high quality modern healthcare (NHS Careers website). This may in part be down to the training for play specialists not yet reaching the level of a degree (level seven on the National Qualification Framework), which interestingly is more commonly the case in other professions allied to medicine (such as the play therapist and psychologist already discussed) and also for hospital play staff working in other countries. As a result there is a resounding discord in that the high level of work undertaken within the play specialist's role is not adequately supported by the necessary level of qualification or training that is required to be registered as an allied health profession.

This said, it is still notable that the professional status and role of play specialists is gaining respect within the health service. The specific recommendation with the National Service Framework for

Children (NSF) that all children in hospital should have daily access to a play specialist (Department of Health 2003) demonstrates this, as does the specific inclusion of qualified play specialists and the work they provide within the Child Health Mapping Service. This is a government-commissioned exercise that aims to create an inventory of all dedicated child health services for the purpose of developing and realizing the aims of the NSF and developing better healthcare services for children and young people.

Promoting wider recognition for the work of play specialists is a priority for many of today's exponents of the ongoing play in hospital movement. The training of play specialists in the UK is on the brink of a major review. The Hospital Play Specialists Education Trust (HPSET), at the time of going to press, were in a period of consultation regarding changes that specifically relate to the training of play specialists, a process that may well see some significant changes likely to occur in the very near future. A higher level of qualification is a likely possibility of such a review. At this point in time, the National Association of Hospital Play Staff (NAHPS) and HPSET, together, have made important headway into entering the complex and lengthy application process involved in being accepted for registration by the Health Professions Council (HPC), the regulatory body for most allied health professions. While the HPC have clearly stated that the level of qualification of play specialists is not a barrier in itself to this registration, a higher level of qualification might still serve to enhance the professional status of play specialists in the UK.

International perspectives

It is interesting to compare and contrast the training and background of play specialists in the UK today with their equivalent counterparts working in healthcare settings in other countries where there is also an established awareness of the need for children to have access to play while they are ill and receiving treatment to improve their health.

In New Zealand, for example, where there is a thriving community of hospital play specialists, the requirements for their practice are a foundation qualification in early years education, potentially followed up with further qualifications in areas such as counselling, psychology or an advanced qualification in education (Hospital Play Specialists Association of New Zealand (HPSANZ) website, www. hospitalplay.org.nz). Once in post, HPSANZ provides ongoing professional development that is particularly relevant to the provision of play for sick children.

Similarly in the United States, a child life specialist, the professional equivalent of the hospital play specialist working in the UK, will have obtained a bachelor or masters degree in 'child life' – the study of child development, family dynamics, individual and group work with children, and incorporating the basic understanding of childhood illnesses alongside certain supervisory, communication and management or leadership skills (University of Akron, Ohio website) – or human development. This will have required the inclusion of an internship or placement in a paediatric healthcare setting, specifically under the supervision of a qualified child life specialist.

Just as in the UK, these countries are home to a healthy community of professionals providing play for sick children in various healthcare settings. It is, however, interesting to witness a greater recognition for the profession and the professionalism of play specialists in these countries, which may be seen as something of a sharp contrast to the situation sometimes faced by play staff in the UK.

Play specialists are not teachers

The hospital education services are provided as part of the Local Education Authority service and seek to have a presence in all children's hospitals and wards. They aim to teach all children with specific medical needs when they are unable to attend school and to provide continuity of education suited to the needs, ability, age and health of children as individuals (Bristol City Council 2009). Hospital-based teachers are fully qualified teaching professionals who work in partnership with children, parents, the child's multi-disciplinary healthcare team and teachers from his or her school in order to minimize the disruption by a period of illness to a child's education. Most children's wards have a schoolroom that is used for some or all of the day and within which school continues to function in as close a way to a normal school classroom as possible.

Children will be taught within the hospital education service when they are expected to be in hospital for five days or more, when short-term hospitalization is part of a prolonged period of absence from school, when they have recurrent admissions to hospital or when they are siblings of long-stay patients even if their education is usually provided by another Local Education Authority (Bristol City Council 2009).

Teachers liaise with a child's school to ensure that his or her educational progress can continue as smoothly as possible through-out his or her hospital stay and period of recovery from treatment. Once children are discharged from their hospital stay, the Hospital Education Service may continue to be involved, providing home edu-cation or – if the child's educational needs or abilities change – refer-ring them to a suitable school or educational unit.

While play specialists may work closely with the hospital school and its teachers, and may very well have a number of shared aims for the child's continued development within the hospital environment, clearly play specialists are not teachers.

Play specialists work differently to play workers

Play workers are specifically trained to work with children and young people in a wide variety of settings. Play work training involves individuals gaining an understanding of child development, the needs and rights of children to be able to access play opportunities and how to encourage children to engage spontaneously and naturally in playful experiences. A significant aspect of the play worker's occupation involves understanding the process of children's play – that is to say how children start or instigate play processes independently or with others, the development and free flow of play activities and how play changes, evolves or ends.

Broadly speaking, the play worker's role is one of facilitator involving the setting up and resourcing of an environment wherein children's play is freely chosen and intrinsically driven (Hughes 1984) and largely untouched by the adults around them. As Brown (2003, p.52) puts it: 'The play worker's role should be taken to include everything necessary to create the conditions that enable children to play'. In contrast, the hospital play specialist aims to guide children to a higher and clearer level of understanding of their experiences by the means of a variety of play techniques.

There are undoubtedly some similarities in the work undertaken by play workers and play specialists, including certain aspects of their training and day-to-day work, such as the facilitation of normal and spontaneous play activities. However a significant way that the role of the play specialist is distinct from that of the play worker is found in the generally non-interventionist role undertaken by play workers (Hughes 1996) as opposed to the often adult-led approach to children's needs utilized by play staff in healthcare settings. Hospital play specialists often use play in a very guided way to bring about a particular outcome, by using play to distract a child through a stressful, invasive procedure or by showing a child what a blood test involves by 'playing it through' using a doll and a book of photo-graphs, for example. It is in this respect that the role of a play worker differs from that of the play specialist specifically trained to work therapeutically with sick children and young people.

Clear professional boundaries within play teams

It is clear that certain misconceptions and confusion can arise in seeking to understand the difference between the role of the play specialist and that of a number of other professionals. However, what might be less clear is that similar issues can arise within play teams, particularly those where there is a combination of senior, junior, trained and untrained team members. This issue may be difficult to manage and can be the cause of significant work stress if it is left unresolved.

As the recognition of play work in hospitals grows, it is becoming increasingly common for play departments to contain a combination of play specialists and play assistants or nursery nurses who work alongside each other. In such departments, there are different respon-sibilities or expectations of each of the team members, depending upon their qualifications and experience. It is the aim of these play departments to provide the best possible service for children and families while they are cared for in hospital. This is usually achieved by the means of employing play assistants (or sometimes nursery nurses) to set up and oversee the provision of normalizing play in a playroom or waiting area, thus enabling the qualified play specialist to take on the more specialized aspects of the role, including prepa-ration for procedures, distraction and support during procedures or treatment and planned one-to-one play sessions intended to help maintain a child's normal development (Walker 2006). Undertaking this more specialized work can often only be possible for play specialists if they have a skilled and capable play assistant working alongside them and maintaining the day-to-day play activities so important to children in hospital. Play assistants may sometimes be able to carry out straightforward preparation or distraction tasks, although these should only really be taken on under the supervision or instruction of a trained play specialist.

Clearly then, there is a need not only to set realistic, reasonable and achieveable professional boundaries so as to keep these two roles separate, but also for the different team members to be able to work effectively within those boundaries. Setting and achieving a good balance within teams is dependent upon good and effective management and open, fair communication, which in itself is no mean feat. Trying to ensure that all team members have a clear, shared vision and understanding of the big picture – of how their service benefits the children in their care – as well as their own role within that big picture should be the aim of those co-ordinating or managing play services for sick children and young people.

The further challenge for the play department is for the professional boundaries between different team members to be understood and respected by other members of the multidisciplinary team. As the fundamental place of hospital play services and the importance of general play within healthcare settings are not universally recognized trying to get colleagues to further understand the differences of individual roles within these services can be something of a significant challenge. A lack of clear understanding about the roles of different individual workers within play teams may have the effect of preventing the appropriate or regular involvement of any play staff with patients. If colleagues are unclear about whom they should ask to carry out different tasks, there is a danger and a likeliness that they will not ask at all.

In spite of a certain amount of necessary overlap, to clarify the different roles of play assistants and play specialists in the most basic of terms, their responsibilities are commonly divided in the following ways:

Play Assistants

☐ normalizing play

☐ maintenance of ward playroom or waiting area

☐ maintenance of toys and equipment

☐ replenishing of supplies

☐ developmental support.

Under the supervision of a trained play specialist:

★ simple distraction

★ simple preparation.

Play Specialists

☐ overseeing normalizing play and often taking a share of the responsibility for the maintenance and replenishing of toys, equipment and supplies as required

☐ developmental support through planned one-to-one or group sessions

☐ preparation for procedures

☐ information sharing about conditions and treatment

☐ distraction and support during treatment or procedures

☐ post-procedural play and support

☐ simple anxiety management

☐ work around phobias or non-compliance.

Play specialists are not babysitters, entertainers or volunteers

In any given setting, it is possible for there to be a number of some-what worrying misconceptions of the role of the ward play special-ist amongst his or her colleagues, patients and their families. These may included a belief that play specialists work predominantly, if not exclusively, with the pre-school children on the ward, or that their main role within the ward is to 'babysit' or entertain children while their parents take a break or when the rest of the ward staff are extremely busy themselves. In addition to these there is a fairly common belief – particularly among parents – that 'the play lady' on the ward is a volunteer. All three of these 'public perceptions' need to be challenged as they unhelpfully hinder the ability to properly fulfil their role on the teams within which they are working.

Play specialists work with children of all ages between birth and 18 years (and sometimes older in the case of some life-limited chil-dren not expected to reach adulthood, who may receive care and support from children's hospices and may also continue to see their consultant or care team into their early adult years). A play specialist's training equips him or her to be able to communicate, adapt work-ing styles and appropriately respond to the needs of children of all ages.

Play specialists may work full or part-time hours. Depending on the setting in which they are based they might work common 'office' hours of 9 a.m. to 5 p.m. from Monday to Friday or they may work a shift pattern similar to that of the nursing staff. Across the board they may be on a variety of different pay bands, but play specialists rarely offer their skills and time voluntarily and are almost all fully employed members of a care team. It is common, however, for the play specialist to work with, manage or to supervise volunteers – specifically selected, willing members of the public – who help out or work alongside them in a ward or playroom setting for a few hours every week.

Where the issues of babysitting and entertaining are concerned, there is a misconception that the play specialist's work is for the purpose only of entertaining, occupying or keeping happy those children unfortunate enough to find themselves unwell and in hospital. Play specialists do indeed provide a variety of fun and entertaining activities and certainly place a high, central value on making it possible for children to access a wide range of normal play activities. However, to see their role purely as being that of entertainer would be to sorely miss the point and significantly underestimate the needs of children for access to play services in hospital. Incidentally, a great many children's wards regularly welcome true entertainers (magicians, storytellers, clowns, etc.) to their playrooms in addition to all the other input they offer to children being cared for within the ward environment. The play specialist may, at times, assist parents by encouraging them to take a well-earned break from the ward environment or caring role by arranging to work with a child at a mutually agreed time, but it is not the role of the play specialist to be used solely or primarily as a babysitter.

One of the most difficult groups of patients, in particular, are those who might be called 'lone' patients. These are children on a ward who are largely unaccompanied for extended periods of time and whose situation presents a challenge to the role of the play specialist because his or her involvement with such children is likely to be generally greater or more intense in the absence of a parental figure. This scenario may result from a variety of circumstances including children whose parents are unable or unwilling to stay with them for long periods of time, possibly because they have other children or commitments away from the hospital. This group may also include children whose parent or carer is also in hospital (this is not uncommon following a traumatic injury such as that sustained in a car accident or house fire), or children who are under a care or protection order while they are in hospital. While these unaccompanied, lone children may demand more supervision and company than other children on the ward it is still not the duty or role of the play specialist to work only with that child or be expected to 'babysit' for him or her. Rather, it is important that the child's needs are carefully considered and assessed alongside all the children on the play specialist's ward or caseload. With good planning, such children would be considered to be a higher priority to the play specialist, who may give more time or playful input to them according to their individual needs. It is not, however, the role of the play specialist specifically to keep them quiet, entertained or happy.

Are play specialists 'play ladies'?!

It's a tough one this, as this is the phrase most commonly used to describe play specialists by the children with whom they work and their families. 'When is the play lady coming round today?', a child may eagerly ask. 'Excuse me, are you the play lady? Please can you come and see my son?', a parent in need of a break or some assistance may enquire. And what about, 'Hello! I'm the play lady on the ward'? Many play specialists use this phrase to introduce themselves and also to describe – arguably not very successfully – what it is that they do and the role they have within the setting where they work.

In general there need not be a problem with the use of this phrase if only because it is fairly inevitable that children themselves will refer to the play specialist by such a term. It is recognized that our job title is somewhat ambiguous in terms of explicitly revealing the role of the hospital play specialist within the ward team and scope of the work that can be delivered. However, it is possible that by assuming the title of 'play lady' play specialists fail to communicate effectively and succinctly to those with whom they work, the role and purpose of that work. Indeed it is possible that it might actually make it less clear to work colleagues, parents and children what play specialists do, as well as why and how the work is done.

It is also possible that there is a risk of somehow 'dumbing down' the importance of the play that is provided for children who are in hospital or have complex health needs. How play specialists choose to describe their work speaks volumes to those around them and can suggest a lack of either clarity or confidence about their own ability or role within a care team – rightly or wrongly – or may even suggest a certain apology or coyness around the role that is certainly not justified.

At a time when play specialists are pushing to gain and retain recognition for their role, it is important to display a confidence and certainty about the what, why and how of this work with sick children, young people and their families. It is also not unreasonable to aim for the development of a sense of pride in their important and often innovative work. The role of the play specialist is highly significant to children and therefore, whether or not this is widely recognized by colleagues, it is important that play specialists should never feel apologetic for what they do but instead should aim to foster the confidence to promote and demonstrate the fundamental benefits of play for the children with whom we work. While the term 'play lady' is snappy and endearing and could be deemed appropriate if being used by children and their families, some caution should be exercised, particularly when in discussion with colleagues.

Some of the difficulties that arise may relate specifically around the job title of play specialist or hospital play specialist. Walker (2006) suggests that some of these difficulties may stem from the use of the word 'play' in the job title, which may serve to suggest a sense of simplicity or innocence that belies the high quality provision that is offered to sick children by trained play specialists. These difficulties may also potentially arise from the fact that many hospital doctors are referred to (if only by the lay-public) as specialists, leading to a degree of confusion first around what play specialists do and also around the level of educational attainment of a play specialist. While this level is often high, it is rarely equal to that of the medical personnel with whom we work. The use of the term 'specialist' certainly does appear to be the cause of some of the difficulties faced as a profession within children's multidisciplinary care teams.

Lansdown (1996) discusses the conundrum over what those who facilitate play should be called and in doing so recognizes the psychological importance of job titles in general, both to the holder of any given title and the perception of others around them. One thing that is for certain is that the roles and responsibilities of play specialists nationwide (not to mention worldwide!) are very diverse, if only because many individual roles have evolved within their own ward-settings as well as the ever-changing wider job profile. While there is some feeling that the job title of 'play specialist' or 'hospital play specialist' is not quite accurate, clear enough, or satisfactory, there is a general agreement that it is extremely difficult to give a single job title that sums up simply what we actually do. 'Play specialist' must therefore suffice for the foreseeable future and will do so if only because the message it clearly gives to all those we work with is that, first and foremost, the basis of our work is play.

SUGAR and SPICE and all things nice: that's what play specialists are made of!

In her book *Helping Sick Children Play*, published in 1980, Barbara Weller presented an acronym that summed up the role of play in hospital in the four following ways:

Participation in play introduces normality in a strange environment

Lessens the impact of pain and anxiety

Allows the child to work through feelings and fears so that hospitalization can become a positive experience

Yields results, recovery is faster and the in-patient stay is reduced. (p.4)

Nearly 30 years on from this, the role of play in hospital remains largely the same, as the following chapters will explore in greater detail. Put simply, play in hospital aims to bridge the gap between the normality of home and the abnormality of the hospital environment. By means of extraordinary skill and the sensitivity to respond to a child's needs, hospital play staff provide a safe space for children to face, work through and learn to cope with the traumatic or unpleasant aspects of illness or hospital treatment. Furthermore, play provision for sick children is known to contribute to shorter in-patient treatment and faster recovery time (Jolly 1976).

Across play work and childcare training generally the functions and benefits of play for children and young people are understood and supported by the acronym 'SPICE' (the pros and cons of using this alone as an approach to play work are discussed by Brown 2003). While in some circles this acronym is considered to be outdated enough to have become obsolete, it does demonstrate at a basic level the areas of development to which play is known to be highly beneficial, and how they are underpinned by playful activities and experiences:

Social interaction

Physical activity

Intellectual stimulation

Creative achievement

Emotional stability.

In the 30 years since Weller presented her acronym, however, hospitals, children and wider recognition of the importance of play – in general development and also specifically for sick children – have seen great change and development. Therefore to deepen and widen understanding of the importance of play in hospital, a further acronym should now be presented in addition to Weller's 1980 original that reflects this move forward accordingly, and also takes into consideration the generally accepted developmental benefits of play (and do note that this should be *in addition*, not in order to replace).

This additional acronym demonstrates the aspects of the role of play specialist that have perhaps become more significant, developed or defined over the 30 years since its predecessor:

Support: cope with stress and trauma caused by illness and hospital experience

Understanding: regarding complex information and ideas

Growth and development: observed and assessed through playful activities

Assessment: children's development, coping ability, level of cognitive ability

Reassure: stability of play environment, body still functional/lost skills.

The constituent parts of this additional descriptor will be explored further and in context within the chapters that follow. However, the basic components of what the play specialist does in the course of his or her work with sick children, in whatever environment this is carried out, can be split into three main areas: the provision of normalizing play; imparting information; and emotional support. The model of the play specialist's practice can therefore be presented as a triangle, made up of these three equal parts (see Figure 2.1). However, the three aspects of the role are not carried out in isolation from each other and each enhances the effects of the other two elements of the play specialist's work. Therefore the model also includes a central area which signifies the areas where these three main elements cross over. This aims to show that when all are included in the play specialist's practice work they bring about the greatest benefit to sick children and young people.

A basic, blank presentation of this model of good practice is shown in Figure 2.1 and will be revisited in later chapters, within which each segment will be more fully described and defined, and by which a fuller picture of good practice will be constructed.

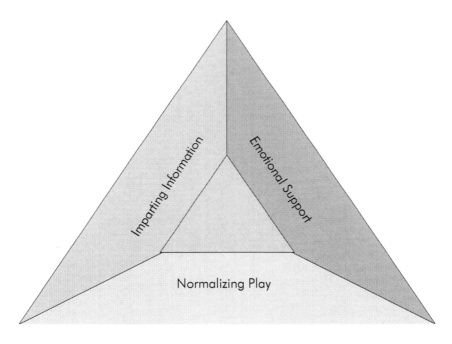

Figure 2.1 The role of the play specialist

3

The Effects of Being in Hospital on Children and Young People

It is never safe to assume that a child will be afraid of an experience that an adult regards as frightening, or conversely that an experience which has no terrors for an adult will have none for a child. (Platt 1959, p.28)

The point from which play specialists generally begin their work with sick children and young people is a basic acceptance that it is normal for children to play and the concern that being physically unwell or spending a period of time in hospital therefore has the potential to interrupt or even harm a child's normal development.

In acceptance of this, play specialists therefore seek through their work with those children to counter some of the stress caused by the difficult, alien and sometimes downright unpleasant experiences of being ill and in hospital. This counteraction is achieved by the provision and encouragement of play – the stimulating, distracting, therapeutic or plain, simple fun that is so normal to the child.

A word about 'normal'

In a world of political correctness, some practitioners may object to or even balk at the idea of using the term 'normal', particularly if it is used specifically in relation to children. While we have managed to modify language used to describe the needs or abilities of others, largely removing that which might be considered offensive or discriminatory – 'handicapped', for example, is now widely recognized as being an unacceptable term – it is often frowned on to use such generalized terms as 'normal', so much so that it has almost been outlawed in some settings. However, this could be seen as an unnecessary reaction, so long as there is some recognition of all that goes into discussing or describing or acknowledging someone or a scenario to be 'normal', or otherwise. It is important to bear in mind that if we consider something 'normal', this judgement is ultimately based on the expectations we have in relation to all that we know about that thing or situation, for instance what we expect of a child 'that age', from 'that background' with 'that kind of issue' in the family.

When thinking about children, then, it is important to set the bar to a reasonable point regarding the debate over whether this term could or should be used. The study of child development, for example, encourages children's practitioners to accept that there is a spectrum of expectations around how children grow, learn, progress and change in all aspects of their lives, behaviour, knowledge and skills. Within such a spectrum it should be accepted that there is a wide middle ground into which the majority of children fall and it is this relatively wide middle of the spectrum that – within this book and the play specialist's practice with children – is to be understood and accepted as being 'normal'. That is to say that, generally speaking, most children at around a particular age, skill level or physical size are expected to be found doing, saying, trying, experiencing and progressing in the same sorts of activities and occupation.

However controversial the use of the term 'normal' may currently be, it is necessary to accept that it is an important term because, by identifying that which is normal, natural, safe, comfortable and secure for most children, play specialists can also skilfully pick up on any deviations from our expectations of the children with whom we work. It is only possibly to identify such difference and variation by understanding the normal expectations of the majority of children (Sheridan 1977).

In addition to this understanding, play specialists base much of their work on the basis that for most children the hospital environment is entirely abnormal compared to their everyday home life and day-to-day activities. While no two homes, families or lifestyles are the same, you can be fairly certain that the sights, sounds, sensations, smells and even the sheer number of people with whom a child interacts when in hospital will be somewhat alien in comparison to his or her 'normal' everyday life. Play specialists therefore aim, through their work with children, to bridge the gaps between the normal, usual and, one hopes, safe and secure environments and experiences of home, school and the individual child's everyday life and the abnormal, threatening, distressing or stressful experiences those children may face during a period of hospitalization or ill health.

Therefore the terms 'normal' and 'abnormal' will be used within this book in spite of the fact that they may not sit entirely comfortably with our politically correct conscience. It is necessary that we acquire a confidence to use and understand these terms given that they provide a relatively firm foundation for understanding the work of the play specialist.

The potential impact of the hospital environment/experience on normal child development

In the not-so-distant past, as we have already seen, there was a significant lack of understanding of the needs of children in hospital. Seen and treated largely as little adults, the role and importance of play, as well as the need for a main caregiver to be present for the wellbeing of the child, was neither fully understood nor appreciated. Today, the extent to which we understand the level of care needed by sick children and young people and their many needs during periods of illness, treatment and recovery has improved greatly. There remains, however, a risk that the interruption by a period of ill health or hospitalization may significantly disturb or detrimentally affect a child's ability to play and maintain his or her normal development. The specific causes for this will be different for individual children and may be many and varied.

It is an important part of the play specialist's work to recognize and anticipate the effects of hospitalization on infants, children and young people and respond to these as effectively as possible. The importance of such provision should be recognized as critical for sick children since the ability to access play can powerfully bridge the gap between maintaining the emotional wellbeing and normal development of the child and the potentially harmful effects of the hospital environment and experience. However, a lack of understanding amongst healthcare staff around the importance of play for sick children or of the scope of the play specialists' role, local variations in the level of priority that is given to play services within multi-disciplinary teams, or a basic lack of resources or finances within healthcare settings can all affect the quality and quantity of play provision for sick children.

In this chapter, by highlighting some of the known effects of hospitalization upon children and young people, and how the play specialist might respond to these, it is hoped that recognition of the need for good play provision in such an environment, supported by trained and knowledgeable play staff, will be brought sharply into focus.

Variations in experiences, stress and children's reactions will arise due to the age of the child and the extent of any trauma or distress caused by his or her illness, treatment and hospital experiences. However, it is recognized that there are some common effects that can be the result of a period of ill health or hospitalization and that all children and young people are at risk of some degree of difficulty as a result of their hospital experience. What follows is an outline of some the difficulties that can present a problem during or after a period of hospitalization or illness and some discussion regarding how play specialists might best respond to the needs of the children affected in such ways. As the needs, abilities and expectations of children generally change throughout childhood, so do the issues they may face as a result of hospitalization. Therefore discussion around these issues and approaches to them has been split into age-specific sections.

The importance of infancy and early experiences, and their effects on development

In the case of babies, there is significant risk that they may seriously fail to have all their needs met during a hospital stay. There is also a particular sense that their development is vulnerable both in the immediate, short term and when looked at with a longer view. Infancy (understood here to refer to a child's first 12 months of life) is the period of life in which children grow faster than they ever will again (Lansdown and Walker 1996). It is a crucial time for bonding between parents and their baby and one that sees enormous change and development. In spite of various schools of research now acknowledging the enormous significance of this time in a child's life, for a very long time the experiences of infants – and the impact of these experiences even on very young babies – were somewhat over-looked. Manning-Morton and Thorp (2003) suggest that the conviction that babies could neither think, reason or know was simply borne out of our inability to ask them about their experiences or understanding of the world or our own inability to remember those things for ourselves. As much more is understood about the significance of early experiences on development as a whole, the case for babies' needs being adequately and appropriately met gathers more and more evidence.

The profound but normal process of growth and development that happens during babyhood therefore requires special recognition and careful consideration when working with babies in hospital. A period of illness can be very stressful for babies and their parents, who may require a lot of support to help them cope as well as possible. It can also impact on their normal development and it is the role of the play specialist always to be mindful of how this can best be supported and enabled to continue as normally as possible given the individual child's circumstances. There especially needs to be due consideration given to babies (as well as in the case of older children) if they are mainly or completely bed-bound, physically restricted by their illness or treatment or without a resident parent or carer, or a combination or all three of these common factors. For this reason, the particular needs of babies in hospital will be looked at in more detail further on this book.

For some babies, particularly those whose period of hospitalization is lengthy, the possibility of a significant interruption to their normal development should present a very real concern to those involved in caring for them. That said, however, even if a baby's stay in hospital is relatively short or straightforward, controversial though it may be to suggest, there is still the potential that those caring for the baby, including play specialists, do not recognize that there could be a more comprehensive response to his or her needs. This may be because the illness of a baby is such that improving his or her physical state supersedes any other area of involvement. In very sick babies, clearly stabilizing their condition is a priority, but once this stability is in place, their needs in other areas of their development and wellbeing also require appropriate and adequate attention and it is here that this is sometimes observed to be somewhat lacking (Yerrell 1998). In addition to the risk of babies not adequately having their needs recognized and met, there is also the very real possibility that those needs may not even be considered to be a priority to play specialists and other healthcare staff. This perception could be result of a number of different issues.

Family self-sufficiency?

One explanation for why play specialists may not necessarily become overly involved in working with babies in hospital (or those being cared for in the community, for example, or another therapeutic setting) is that these children often have at least one parent permanently staying with them. That parent may want to care as fully as possible for their sick baby – and probably will be being encouraged to do so (as per the guidelines of many government discussions regarding families of sick and disabled children). It is, however, sometimes possible to perceive that families of sick babies need more space and less involvement from play staff than those with older children. This perceived level of involvement and the attention they want or need may, in reality, differ considerably – frequently families would like more involvement with the play specialist than may appear to be the case. Furthermore, it is significantly more often the case than not that all children in hospital have at least one parent staying with them permanently. This is not, however, usually deemed to be a reason why play staff should not have some involvement with children in hospital. There is no more reason for this to be the case for babies than for any other child being looked after during a period of illness.

Families of babies in hospital, especially (but not exclusively) where this is their first baby, may actually need a significant amount of support and involvement from staff, including the play specialist. This may be either because they themselves are unsure of how to respond to their baby's needs, and the ways in which these may have changed during a period of illness, or because they are struggling with their own distress caused by the difficulties of their situation. Having a new baby can be daunting and overwhelming at the best of times without the added stresses caused by that baby being unwell and in need of specialized care.

As a result it is probably worth assuming (until proven otherwise) that all families in this position will be in need of a considerable amount of support and as much encouragement (and possibly instruction) to help them to continue to feed (if possible), bond with and care for their poorly babies. In families where the sick baby is not their only child, parents may only be able to visit for limited periods of time on a daily basis or less, or there may be a number of siblings present on the hospital ward for extended amounts of time. In both of these situations the input of the play specialist may be invaluable in a variety of ways. An important part of the play specialist's role for these families could be to promote, through various aspects of her work, the positive, affectionate interactions between babies, their parents and carers that underpin good bonding and attachment and to enable that child's development to continue as naturally and normally as possible in spite of his or her illness.

'Auto-pilot' development?

Another reason for this lack of involvement may be a mistaken belief that a child's development happens so automatically in his or her early years that specialized input is not wholly necessary or of value. Therefore it might be thought that there is not a clear enough reason for specific involvement by the play specialist. However, as research into child development has progressed, a basic view of strict Piagetian stage development (i.e. 'A at age X is followed by B which is in turn followed by C around age Y and then D') – which may contribute to this belief – has been widely disputed and therefore is somewhat less influential than it used to be when considering children's abilities and needs.

Through research we are becoming increasingly aware of the complexity and rapidity of children's development in the first three years of life (Manning-Morton and Thorp 2003). It is becoming more apparent that a great many things influence the development of children on a very individual basis, having both positive and negative implications, depending on their early life experiences. Children develop and respond differently to various situations because the early experiences of individuals greatly influence and affect how they will cope through the course of life.

What is most important to accept when engaging with babies is the issue of potential. It is no longer acceptable to view every child's development as merely a uniform journey, passing the same landmarks and points at which the same responses and observations are made. Rather it is more appropriate to accept that children are all born with the potential to develop normally and to the best of their own individual ability. This optimal development, however, requires appropriate and effective support, affection, stimulation and care – and it is the need for that input that is really the pertinent issue here.

Do babies really need play?

A further view of work with babies is a perception, acknowledged particularly within daycare settings, that play work with babies and toddlers is not deemed valuable because many adults still believe that babies do not or cannot really play (Manning-Morton and Thorp 2003). It is possible that this view could affect the play specialist's drive to become involved in working with sick babies, and could also affect the likelihood of parents or other healthcare staff requesting such involvement. Research into baby activity and development (including that by Dunn 1988, Gopnik, Meltzoff and Kuhl 1999 and Goldschmied and Jackson 2004), has shown that babies can and do play, that their play has great value in terms of the enrichment of their lives and that it greatly supports that overall development. Furthermore, where play is concerned – as with all their other needs – the physical dependence of babies means that they rely on those who care for them 'to bring the world to them and them to the world' (Manning-Morton and Thorp 2003, p.13). Without the provision of play and opportunities to experience the new and wondrous world around them, babies' experiences of the many environments around them would be sorely lacking in anything of much meaning.

It has always been the suggestion of psychoanalytical theory (such as that first put forward by Sigmund Freud) that all of a child's early experiences will significantly affect his or her development, regardless of whether he or she retains any memory of specific events. Scientific research into brain development in more recent times now offers some solid evidence that this is indeed the case and not merely psychological supposition (Eliot 1999). It therefore should be accepted that everything a baby hears, sees, touches, tastes and smells as well as all of a baby's movements and experiences whether passive or active all contribute to the way the brain grows (Jolly 1981; Batmanghelidjh 2006), and makes connections, and ultimately how a child grows to experience and cope with the world.

This point in particular is highly significant when we consider the infant in hospital and all that he or she may experience. The biggest concerns of those involved in working with sick babies should ultimately be the support and achievement of as normal a development as possible. By means of a detailed understanding of child development, being able to identify the particular needs of the babies in their care and by working well across the multidisciplinary team, the play specialist can plan and provide play and respond to babies in a way that is both effective and preventative and that aims for the maintenance and protection of a child's optimal development. The involvement of play specialists with babies in this way therefore has an important role in countering some of the potentially harmful effects that may come from the experience of being in hospital.

When considered in the light of this observation, the needs of babies who are sick and in hospital are profound. In this situation, simply by being unwell, this crucial time of change, discovery and exciting experiences so central to a child's development is already put in a position of risk. By the limitations placed upon an infant when sick and requiring specialized care in hospital, there is a distinct risk that all those things that are central to all areas of their development will be disturbed, neglected and, in the worst-case scenario, impaired. If, in response to this risk, there is a lack of recognition of the needs of babies when they are in hospital or an insufficient or ineffective response is made to these needs, the greater the likelihood is that their development, ability to make attachments or emotional wellbeing will be adversely affected.

As asserted by Manning-Morton and Thorp (2003), a significant feature pertaining to babies in hospital – and indeed in general – is that they are completely dependent upon the adults around them to support, encourage and provide for their development and overall wellbeing. The helplessness of infants makes them especially vulnerable. Provision that meets their needs as fully as possible should therefore be a priority for the play specialist.

The danger resulting from this vulnerability is threefold. There is a misconceived belief that babies are relatively unresponsive to any play work that is offered and therefore may not require a considerable amount of support. This could be compounded by the misguided opinion – raised by Manning-Morton and Thorp (2003) – that babies do not play, as previously discussed in this chapter. Conversely, it could be perceived that the needs of babies are in fact too complex to be adequately met by the work offered by play staff. Equally, work with babies may sometimes be overlooked because it seems easier to work with or provide play for toddlers and older children. This could be because they are more able to vocalize their needs, to make choices and be self-motivated in their play activities. With babies, play requires a more overtly therapeutic approach that is both completely motivated and facilitated by their supporting adults and that is concerned with assessing and supporting a child's development. Indeed, all that a baby experiences has an impact on his or her development one way or another (Batmanghleidjh 2006; Gerhardt 2004) which means that any play provision offered should be well considered and, where possible, well planned.

Given the potential for these pre-conceived ideas of working with babies as well as the need to carefully consider their multifaceted needs, it is understandable that play staff could find the prospect of working with some very young patients somewhat daunting. This can result in the work of play specialists with these patients becoming diminished to all but a bare minimum. The potential outcome of such minimal involvement is that these tiny children and their families may see relatively little of the play specialist – busy with other patients – apart from perhaps a daily, 'Hi there and hello!' and are provided with a minimal amount of toys or equipment.

These resources are likely to be items such as a baby gym, mobile or light projector which can be set up and left for periods of time and of which babies are largely forced to be passive observers. They are deceptive resources because they usually give the illusion of being an engaging and interactive toy from which babies will gain pleasure and stimulation. Caution therefore should be exercised when selecting resources for use with babies. It is simply not enough to hand resources such as these to families, believing that this constitutes adequate 'play provision'. The provision of play for sick children, and babies in particular, is as much – or more, in fact – to do with relationships and interaction as it is about resources and playthings.

Manning-Morton and Thorp (2003) emphasize that a key feature of the emotional and physical dependence of very young children is the relationship that is formed between 'practitioner' and child, as well as supporting precious bonds between a baby and his or her parents, especially the mother. Gerhardt is in agreement with this opinion and observes that babies need, in a sense, to be invited to participate in human culture – they cannot begin to engage, participate and develop by their own means alone. It is Gerhardt's assertion that the first important step in this process is to 'get the baby hooked on social interaction itself by making it highly pleasurable' (Gerhardt 2004, p.39).

Accepting, then, that babies' needs are relatively profound, as is dictated by their vulnerability and dependence upon others, in order to meet their fundamental needs, the response of the play specialist needs to be one of proactive, positive and effective involvement, rather than avoidance or the minimal provision of unhelpful resources. The play specialist needs to be aware of the development that happens in a child's vital first 12 to 18 months, the significance of attachment and bonding, how these could be disrupted or indeed damaged by the experience of hospitalization in infancy and how best to prioritize and provide for the needs of such young children. What follows, therefore, is an outline of what are considered to be the central needs of babies in hospital and some discussion around how best the play specialist involved in their care might provide play-based activities in response to those needs.

 For parents to be adequately supported, helped and encouraged to bond with and to care for their baby as naturally as possible

Having a young baby to care for can be a stressful, tiring and worrying time for any parent, without the added strain of that baby being unwell and requiring care in hospital. When this situation is added into the mix, parents can be expected to be anxious, emotional and sometimes impatient or angry. In the hospital environment with a specialized team caring for their sick baby, parents can sometimes struggle with a sense of having no control over their lives and their child's care, having lost their role as parent and carer, and even have feelings of being useless or 'in the way' (Yerrell 1998).

In 1959, the Platt Report acknowledged that where at all possible the admission of mothers to hospital with their infants was of value so that they could continue as far as possible to care for them. Nowadays it is almost exclusively the case that parents of sick babies (particularly mothers) are resident in hospital during their admission and yet they can feel very out of their depth in trying to maintain as far as possible any normal day-to-day life for their child. They might be nervous of medical equipment and treatment and may fear that their usual care will somehow jeopardize the efforts of the healthcare team, or they may simply be in a state of shock or distress at the situation.

Staff caring for babies in hospital need to be aware of the stress that can tell heavily on parents at this time. This needs to be acknowledged if only because that stress can be communicated to the baby, who in turn may suffer from the negative effects of stress (Lansdown 1996; Gerhardt 2004). They should also make it a priority to enable parents to continue to care for their baby as normally as is at all possible and should receive all the support necessary to do so. This support may involve simply talking about parents' feelings of stress or anxiety and actively listening to their concerns. Within the play specialist's role, this will involve encouraging play, interaction, close physical contact and talking between parents and their baby. In the special case of mothers who wish to continue breastfeeding their baby, this may be enabled by the provision of equipment such as feeding cushions or breast pumps.

To be held and touched – skin-to-skin, stroking, rocking, patting, massage

Babies respond significantly to touch right from the moment they are born (Gerhardt 2004) and particularly benefit from close, secure holding when they are distressed or in need of comfort. Therefore where at all possible, parents should be encouraged and enabled to hold and cuddle their babies as much as possible. In order for this to happen, they may need reassurance or instruction over how to negotiate any dressings or intravenous lines currently adorning their baby's tiny body. If holding a baby is not possible because he or she is simply too unwell to be moved or handled in this way, parents should be encouraged to stroke or gently pat their baby as he or she lies in the cot. Some young babies respond positively to patting, finding it soothing and calming, possibly because it is reminiscent of being close to a rhythmical heartbeat in the womb.

 To be talked to – talking, singing, use of his or her name

From birth (or very shortly afterwards) babies can recognize their parents' voices, and prefer these to any other sound they hear (Lansdown and Walker 1996; Gerhardt 2004). While his or her sight is a foggy jumble for quite some weeks, a baby's hearing is acute and discerning, even at a very young age. Therefore it is understandable that what he or she hears can be very powerful. The noises a baby may hear in hospital – alarms, buzzers, many different people talking – could become a very unfamiliar and disturbing jumble. Therefore talking or singing to babies in hospital is important, as is encouraging their parents to do so. A child's name is a sound that with continual use and repetition the child will begin to recognize as significant to him- or herself. In an environment that can be impersonal and clinical, to use a baby's name serves to remind everyone that 'baby' is more than just 'baby' and certainly is more than a physical problem or condition.

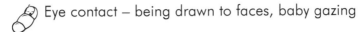

Eye contact – being drawn to faces, baby gazing

Eye contact between babies and their parents (particularly mothers) is a central part of the bonding process (Gerhardt 2004). Babies are naturally drawn to look at faces from birth, even while their eyesight is still relatively poor. Their ability to perceive and receive information from facial expressions and eye contact is a key way that children learn about the world and relationships. Parents equally can seem to spend hours simply looking at their baby, yet this 'baby gazing' should be accepted as being a key part to the parents' process of falling in love with their children.

Recognition by healthcare staff of an appropriate level of stimulation

Babies in hospital are at risk of being either over-stimulated or under-stimulated. Over-stimulation can occur when there is too much sensory arousal from external sources. In hospital a baby may be examined or handled a great deal at times, he or she may experience pain or discomfort, there may be loud or strange noises fairly constantly and there may be a lack of natural light or darkness (artificial lighting may mean it is constantly relatively light, even at nighttime). Under-stimulation, at times, is as much of a risk, as has already been suggested above, especially if there is a minimal amount of involvement from multidisciplinary team members including the play specialist. This could equally be a problem if the resources on offer to babies require them to be very passive or to look continually at the same objects for hours on end. Babies benefit most from interaction with other people who can strike the right balance and by gauging how much to stimulate or excite them and when to soothe and calm them.

Appropriate support to progress and develop as normally as possible

By their knowledge and skills in child development and by being able to judge and respond appropriately to the needs of children, play specialists should be able to offer a good mix of activities. Some of these can be left with parents who in turn may be encouraged by the play specialist to interact and play with their child. Others may form a one-to-one session with a baby, with or without his or her parents present. By communication within the multidisciplinary team, the play specialist will have identified the specific needs of the babies for whom he or she is involved in caring and will be able to plan for how best to meet these needs with the resources available.

 Opportunities to wonder and experience the world using all of the senses

With a broad understanding of play types and their various benefits, play specialists will not only plan play sessions that serve to support an infant's continuing development, but also understand the significance that babies need play to be taken to them in order for them to engage with and enjoy new, exciting experiences. Even if babies are bed-bound or restricted by their condition or its treatment, the play specialist can help them to experience as much as possible by providing a wide variety of play activities, which are fun, joyful and pleasurable.

Caring for babies in hospital – in every aspect of that care – requires something of a high level of skill and the work of the play specialist involved with sick babies is by no means an exception to this. The

complexity of the needs presented by the youngest patients, however, should not be the cause of minimal or ineffective provision for those needs. Rather, the knowledge and skills of the play specialist in recognizing and responding to the needs of sick children – even when they are very young – should mean that babies' development and precious attachments to their parents can be protected and allowed to continue in a way that is as normal as possible within the constraints of their illness, its treatment and the restrictions of being in hospital.

Young children in hospital

A significant number of young children will experience an admission to hospital during their early years. Statistics from 1993 suggested that around 10 per cent of children under five were admitted to hospital (Lansdown 1996) although our understanding of what is meant by the term 'admission' in this case is somewhat woolly. No significant information is given, for example, regarding the length of stay or interventions carried out during that time. In correlation with these numbers, a later study of the statistics regarding hospital admissions between 1990 and 1997 showed an increase in the number of children spending time in hospital from 85 children (aged under five years) to 100 per 1000 children (National Statistics Online 2004).

It is perhaps not unfair to observe that 10 per cent of the nation's toddlers and pre-schoolers is a significant chunk of the population. While that is the number admitted to hospital, understood here to mean 'to *stay* (having been allocated a bed) for some time', we can assume that a great many more are seen and given treatment in the Outpatient and Accident and Emergency departments. Furthermore, it is not unreasonable to state that all small children, at some stage, will receive treatment or consultation in healthcare or walk-in centres or general practice clinics.

An intense and exciting time in children's lives, toddlerdom and the pre-school phase is a period of extensive change that involves relatively enormous physical growth and the mastery of complicated physical ability, from walking, running and jumping to early writing skills. It is during this time that children really progress from being a baby to a little person in their own right through the acquisition of language skills, by gaining a degree of control over their own bodily functions, by learning about choice and autonomy over their activities and therefore by being better able to express their own wants and needs. It is also a time when children face the complex task of beginning to develop an understanding of the social world around them and how to interact with others – as well as how not to! – whilst constantly experiencing and gaining some control over the intensity of their own feelings.

This age is also a time where play is central to the child's experience of the world (Lansdown and Walker 1996). A self-motivated and fun-filled activity, it is also the means by which little children are able to explore, experiment, practise skills and challenge just about anything and everything. By being enabled to partake in playful activities, over which they have the freedom to make choices, they can explore and experiment with the world around them and in doing so discover strategies for coping with the everyday problems life throws their way. By the provision of playful activities and open access to a space within which children are encouraged to play freely, a child's own comforting and familiar activities can continue as normally as possible. By allowing and encouraging normalizing play of this nature, it is hoped that young children will cope as well as possible with the sometimes stressful or distressing experience of being ill and in hospital. The involvement of the play specialist is also important for children within this age group. Communication, understanding and relationship building are already naturally explored and achieved by children through play. Alongside the normalizing play facilitated by the play specialist, young children can be helped by her work to cope with the more difficult aspects of a period of illness.

Don't leave me...!

Where children under the age of five are concerned, there is a generally good understanding amongst healthcare professionals of the potential for a period of hospitalization to create disturbances in their attachments with their main carers. The work of James and Joyce Robertson, if nothing else, highlighted this to be an area of great significance. The resulting concern for assisting children in maintaining close contact with their parents during their hospital stay has become an important aspect in the training of paediatric healthcare professionals. It is very common, in a variety of settings, for little children around this age to struggle with insecurity associated with an actual or perceived separation from Mum or Dad. This anxiety can become more acute in the context of a hospital stay in an environment that can be bewildering, with many new faces in addition to the experience of feeling unwell and possibly having to cope with invasive medical treatment or procedures.

This sense of anxiety can show itself in a variety of different ways in children still too young to reliably express their feelings and their needs verbally. Significantly, regression can become an issue for the under-fives (Lansdown 1996). Clinginess and insecurity around being left, even for very short periods of time, are also signs of regression that can be distressing for the whole family (Jolly 1981). Very little children are commonly seen to become overly clingy towards their parents or main carer and also are capable of becoming much more tearful or grizzly than usual. They might display restless or hyperactive behaviour or may alternatively become withdrawn and overly quiet.

Signs of regression may also be observed, for example, in a child who has recently acquired bowel and bladder control. A child who has been clean and dry at least during the day may begin soiling and wetting again, both to the concern of parents and potentially to the distress of the child. Reassurance should be made that this is quite common and usually only a temporary problem that resolves itself once the child recovers from his or her illness and begins to resume a restored or more normal routine or lifestyle.

In addition to a lack of bowel or bladder control, little children may display new or increased tendencies towards self-soothing behaviour such as thumb-sucking, hair pulling or 'twiddling', nail biting, nose picking or even masturbation. None of these behaviours necessarily poses a problem in isolation or in the short term, particularly if they are not considered to be in the extreme. However, it is important that all those involved in the care of sick children are aware of the signs that may suggest a sense of stress, anxiety or distress or show that a child is trying to cope or soothe him- or herself. Intervention by the play specialist or other professionals such as psychologist, art or music therapist on acknowledging such self-soothing behaviour may be useful in helping to alleviate a child's stress and better foster good coping strategies.

Up for the challenge?

While the many and varied signs of regression are cause for concern to those working with sick children, it would be short-sighted to think that bonding and clinginess are overriding issues facing toddlers and pre-schoolers. Just as their lives involve many complex aspects of social and personal development, the experience of a period of ill health or hospitalization can have an effect upon many other areas of their development or wellbeing.

The toddler years can be characterized as a time when children begin to assert their independence. When unwell and perhaps receiving treatment in hospital this newly discovered independence can be taken from the child in a variety of ways (Lansdown 1980) – from the physical constraints of illness or treatment to being stripped of the safe and comforting routine and environment of home. This loss of independence and control can be distressing and frustrating for little children, and may lead to difficult behaviour. It is common for toddlers and pre-school-age children to show their anger and distress at the new and strange experience of being ill and in hospital by demonstrating an increase in tantrums and clinginess, and a return to babyish behaviour, as already discussed.

It is helpful to recognize that toddler and pre-school years commonly bring with them difficult, unpredictable and somewhat ritualistic behaviour (Lansdown and Walker 1996). Therefore those working with children in potentially stressful healthcare environments should keep an open mind around challenging behaviour, not necessarily attributing all difficult behaviour observed to the child's illness or treatment. It is perhaps a good idea to exercise some caution before launching in and flagging up a serious concern at the first hurdle encountered with a child. Unless serious problems are clear, it is always advisable to spend time observing and getting to know a child and his or her family, if necessary taking note of any observations that may prove to be of significance.

Many very little children appear to need or rely upon a sense of routine, normality, safety and familiarity in terms of their immediate environment, activities and trusted carers. The young child's need for security, coupled with his or her need to control their environment while testing the boundaries of this control, can be difficult and extremely stressful for families to manage even without the additional stress of a period of illness or hospitalization. Add to a child's already challenging behaviour the experience of having to spend some time in hospital – a new, threatening and strange environment with many new people – and some families may struggle to cope, requiring a greater degree of support from those involved with them and their child.

By becoming familiar with what is normal and acceptable for individual children, in terms of behaviour (as well as other aspects of their development, as has already been discussed), not only do play specialists get to know their patients on a closer level, but they will be able to offer a more meaningful level of support and reassurance to families. Part of their role can be to help families – and indeed colleagues – to understand what behaviour might fall within the realms of a 'normal' reaction to a stressful experience and what can be done to assist the whole family to cope with the hospital treatment.

I'm not a baby any more! Issues in middle childhood

During middle childhood – that is between five and eleven years – some of those difficulties encountered by toddlers and pre-school children can be more easily overcome, if only because children have by then gained a greater capacity for learning, understanding and expressing themselves more effectively through language. However, they are potentially as vulnerable as younger children within the hospital environment as it is still an environment that is very different and daunting compared to their everyday home and school life – at least in the main. Increased independence from parents and family will be more established and comfortable when all is going well in life, but children may still struggle significantly when the stability provided by home, school and family is interrupted or threatened by a period of illness with or without hospitalization (Jolly 1981).

Children of this age may be just as needy, clingy or insecure as their toddler-age counterparts and this may be a great challenge to either the family or hospital staff who may have quite rigid age-related expectations of children as they get older. It may also be distressing for children themselves who are not only fearful in response to the situation itself, but also fear the new emotions they are experiencing as a result of their current feelings of insecurity. They may also fear ridicule or resent being treated in an inappropriate manner by others.

Fears and fantasies

Within this period of childhood – in particular from around five to eight years – children's thinking is still very much influenced by their own fantasy and make-believe thoughts. Therefore children in hospital are very much at risk of fantasizing elaborate thoughts not only about why they are ill or injured, but also how they are to be treated and made better or how long they may have to stay as an inpatient. Even if children of this age have begun to gain a more concrete sense of biology and how their bodies work, without an appropriate amount of support and information from those caring for them, including their parents, these children may struggle with a strong sense of uncertainty and fear. They are at risk of experiencing great anxiety by imagining what might happen to them during treatment for their illness.

If a child is going to have his tonsils taken out, for example, while he might understand that tonsils are located in the throat and need to be removed to prevent further ill health, he may imagine that in order to get to them, the doctors will need to cut off his head. Equally a child who needs to have her appendix removed may fear that her body will be broken or work less effectively by this loss of a body part – albeit an unnecessary one (Jolly 1981). This and similar thoughts may be frightening to a point where a child feels overwhelmed by anxiety. Cook (1999) gives a similar example of an eight-year-old boy who experienced distress by his misunderstanding of the drainage tubes that were in situ following surgery. The child 'had been watching the blood-stained serous fluid passing down the tube and was afraid that his body was "melting" and disappearing into the bag at the side of his bed' (p.39). A basic awareness and acceptance that such fantasies exist and may cause children difficulties should always be at the back of the play specialist's mind when getting to know children and planning work with them. The level of reassurance required by such children must not be underestimated and certainly should be a high priority to the play specialist.

Children in this age group may still struggle to communicate their worries over such things verbally, although this is a period of childhood where children become more able to express their needs, thoughts and feelings in a more effective and mature way. They may, however, simply be too frightened to express how they are feeling, either because they may believe that by voicing such fear it will be made all the more real, or because they are afraid of looking or feeling silly by discussing their thoughts with others. Fears of this nature may therefore be expressed, at least in part, through challenging behaviour or by refusing to comply with the requests of medical and nursing staff. Play specialists may need to approach these children sensitively in order to establish whether they are struggling with fears or anxieties that may be underlying such behaviour. At this age, especially if their understanding of bodily functions is still relatively basic, there is a significant danger that explanations for illness that are produced from their own imagination will be way off target.

Discussions with children about and throughout their illness, treatment and recovery require a level of skill and sensitivity that will ensure that adequate and appropriate information is given to 're-align' children's understanding and that further fear and fantasizing is therefore avoided (see Chapter 6: 'Imparting Information').

In attempting to make sense of their confusion around being unwell, children may perceive illness or injury to be a punishment for bad or silly behaviour or by the bidding of someone or something else. This belief may be intensified if they were warned against a certain activity or behaviour, which then resulted in them being hurt or becoming unwell. This theory of 'imminent justice' – discussed by Lansdown (1996) – is thought particularly to form part of the thought processes of younger children aged between about four and seven years old. Between the ages of eight and ten years, generally speaking however, children have a more concrete understanding of their body and bodily functions and a greater sense of cause and effect and they are therefore more able to acknowledge that illness as a punishment or by human will actually constitutes rather a poor explanation. They are much more able to take on board factual explanations that aid understanding of their condition and its treatment.

Independence days

Between the ages of about eight and eleven years old, life is an exciting time of developing new physical skills. The experience of being ill and in hospital may serve to undermine a child's sense of fulfilment, achievement and self-esteem. The loss of such skills or abilities, even if this loss is temporary and even if the ability is only slightly affected, may lead to a child experiencing very real fears that his or her body is broken and unable to function. Since so much of their time is normally spent at school or engaged in activities with other children of a similar age, these children may also struggle with a sense of isolation from their friends and usual social activities that is the result of being ill and possibly having to stay in hospital. Feelings of isolation and of missing their friends may add to the fears encountered by children within this age group not only that their bodies do not work effectively but also that this has led to a restriction of their normal routine and daily activities. Such fears may show themselves through behaviour, which may indicate that they are feeling frustrated, sad, angry or they may even show some signs that suggest that they are feeling quite depressed, such as being withdrawn and disconnected to the world around them or tearful.

A feature of this period of time might also be seen to be an increased sense of independence from their parents. That said, children do still remain reliant on their parents for support in most, if not all areas of their lives during this time. For children of this age, a period of illness that causes their skills and abilities to be impaired by illness or injury may be the source of significant frustration and distress. They may also, in a sense, grieve for the perceived loss of their growing sense of independence upon which they are just embarking.

In the case of children who are struggling with this sense of loss as a result of being unwell, play can be used to good effect in order to reassure them that their bodies still work, that they are still in possession of skills and that they can indeed continue to make progress in their development. Following an assessment of the circumstances and needs of individual children, play specialists can provide input and activities that can help them to achieve manageable goals and in doing so boost their own sense of self-esteem. The role of a play specialist can include assisting children in expressing anger and frustration at their situation relatively safely. This may simply be through encouraging and allowing children to talk about their feelings or may include games involving throwing or punching, large-scale art activities or sessions using playdough or clay that will allow a child to transfer and thus release some of his or her physically held anger.

Furthermore, by working with other members of the multidisciplinary team, play specialists can also work towards helping children regain some of their lost physical skills through specific set activities. They might work alongside a child's physiotherapist, for example, and aim to encourage that child to sit or stand in a position that is recommended, or practise a specific exercise that can be incorporated into the play activities provided. (See the example given of Edward in Chapter 4 about the importance of normalizing play.)

In addition to the acquisition of physical skills, this age group of children can be seen to take on a large amount of new knowledge and it is a time when conceptual thinking becomes more mature. While this acquisition of knowledge must be encouraged, celebrated and supported, caution must be taken when working with seemingly very knowledgeable children. Much as they might be able to spout off many facts and figures about their condition and treatment with alarming accuracy, on further investigation some children continue to be quite uncertain about why they are ill and how their treatment is working. Children can become highly adept at overhearing and repackaging information, without necessarily having gained a clear understanding of all the detail that they appear to have taken in. Establishing what they actually know and where there are gaps in their knowledge may require a careful unpicking of the facts of which they are in possession. This will, in turn, allow an appropriate and acceptable level of support and information to be offered to the child, facilitating much-needed reassurance for the child who will, in turn, gain a better level of understanding about his or her condition and its treatment.

Knowing and understanding: cognitive development issues in early childhood

While the areas of knowing, understanding and taking on new information will also be looked at in Chapter 6 of this book, in trying to understand what the experience of being in hospital can be like for children it is important to acknowledge the role that cognitive development can have in that experience. Children's limited understanding of events, concepts and time in particular has the potential to significantly affect how they experience illness, healthcare settings and any treatment they are given and also how they respond to those involved in caring for them.

The concept of time can be difficult for children to fathom, as can ideas around cause and effect, but these can significantly affect how well children manage the experience of being ill, especially if they are being cared for in hospital. Young children in particular are seen to live very much 'in the moment' and cannot make sense of any long stretches of time, especially if they cannot be broken down into more imaginable chunks. Some children can be helped to understand how long their hospital stay may be, for example, by explaining that they will be staying for 'x number of sleeps'. This approach will only be useful though if the child is able to count, is able to imagine what that amount of sleeps – and the stretches of time in between those 'sleeps' – will be like, and as long as the amount of nights described is limited to a manageable amount, and is a realistic estimate. Some children will hold their parents to ransom over the number of nights promised and will not cope well if the actual number is subject to a change. Where possible and where a child's capacity is judged as capable of taking on such information, time should be broken into understandable chunks. However, this will only be helpful if it is not going to present children with more information of which they cannot make sense. If it is unnecessary or impossible to give a reliable sense of time to a child, regarding his or her treatment or admission to hospital, then it is probably best not to embark on such information in the first place. It is a much better aim to work with children where they are often most comfortable – in the here and now.

Studies now dating back some 25 years suggest that in this period of childhood, children's understanding of health, bodily functions and illness means that they perceive ill health to be the result of contagion or a variety of external factors (Bibace and Walsh 1981). The majority of these studies were based on the Piagetian view of child development previously discussed and may therefore now be called into question due to Piaget's theories on how children learn and develop having been the subject of significant challenge. That said, however, more independent studies into this area of cognitive development do consistently seem to suggest that children's understanding of health and illness appears to develop in systematic and predictable sequence (Eiser 1981, cited in Meadows 1993).

Babies are very interested in their own bodies and explore them frequently. As they approach their first birthday, they begin to be able to point when prompted to various body parts (Young 2007).

Further awareness of their bodily functions usually starts to emerge between 12 and 24 months, with an increased interest in investigating all that their bodies produce and often heralding the beginning of toilet training! Very young children live very physical lives and their bodies are a source of constant fascination. By the time they embark on their school days most children have gained a rudimentary knowledge of the contents of their bodies, particularly understanding that they contain brain, blood, bones and a heart, and that when they eat their food travels into their stomach (Meadows 1993), but little else about the more complicated inner workings of their bodies.

Undoubtedly then, it is the case that within this period of early childhood, children reliably know some solid, basic facts about their bodies, confirmed by simply observing children and asking them simple questions about themselves. What can be difficult, however, is to grasp an accurate picture of what children really understand about how their bodies work. This difficulty is often a result of children being less able to express themselves verbally, and not necessarily because they are fundamentally unable to process complicated information (Lansdown 1996; Lansdown and Walker 1996). Moreover, in the context of the play specialist's work, it can be difficult to ascertain what children understand about how the body functions and what it means for part of the body to no longer work effectively or for it to become impaired by accident or illness.

The exception to this might be the case of children who have a long-term, chronic or life-threatening illness. A group of children being treated for leukaemia were studied in great detail by Myra Bluebond-Langner in the late 1970s. In discussing the observations made within her work, Bluebond-Langner (1978) states that even children as young as two or three years old have a degree of understanding about death, shown in the way they 'fantasize and are concerned about dying' (p.50). Her observation continues in suggesting that very sick children, such as those with whom she had spent a great deal of time observing, would have 'even more cause' to be aware and concerned with their illness and possibly with death because of their experiences during their hospital treatment. This statement has been debated and disputed (Lansdown 1996), but at the very least provides food for thought for those working with sick children in a variety of settings.

In spite of the observations of Bluebond-Langner, it is more commonly understood to be the case that children under the age of around seven years have a growing, yet somewhat incomplete understanding of the issues affecting them during a period of illness or treatment in hospital. They are, however, continually learning from and exploring information and experiences not only of the world around them, but of their own bodies. Their knowledge and understanding of how their body functions is always expanding little by little and a period of illness, if handled sensitively, can be a time when that knowledge expands and deepens.

The play specialist's aim should therefore always be to establish a baseline understanding of what each individual child with whom he or she works knows about his or her body, illness and treatment. This point is found to recur again and again throughout this book – with good reason, as this approach is a key feature of much if not all of the work carried out by play specialists.

Teenagers in hospital

When we come to consider the effects of being in hospital on teenagers and their needs during a time of illness, we need first to accept that adolescents are different to children because they are negotiating a different developmental stage to those children that they once were. Because of this reality, the care they receive when they are unwell needs to reflect this difference.

In the past, it was often assumed that adolescents – well on the road to adulthood – were just as able to cope with difficult or unfamiliar situations as adults would and if admitted to hospital, were regularly cared for in an adult setting. However, teenagers are also distinct from adults because they are still in the process of maturation and development. This difference must also be reflected in any package of care they receive within the health services.

In the light of these statements then, it is worth considering what is meant and understood by 'adolescence', since this is a term that can take on many and varied meanings from person to person. Do we, for example, define adolescence as a physical stage of growth and change? Do we place a beginning and end point to this life stage according to age? Does it have more to do with the acquisition of knowledge, of skills, or of responsibility? Is it a time that starts only once a person's sexual development begins, or that ends once a sense of identity and a place in a given society or culture is achieved? Ask a hundred people to define the beginning and the end of adolescence and it is likely that a hundred different explanations would be presented.

Lansdown and Walker (1996) suggest that it is necessary to make a distinction between 'puberty' and 'adolescence'. Both terms are often incorrectly understood to mean one and the same thing, but in fact denote two very different processes of change. Puberty is more helpfully understood as a series of physical and physiological changes, including relatively rapid growth, changes in the proportions of the body and the development of sex organs and sexual characteristics. All these changes act to convert children into adults who themselves are capable of sexual reproduction. Adolescence on the other hand should be understood to mean the whole process of growing up in all the areas that are included in that transition – physical, psychological, social and cultural. This all-encompassing process of change is much more lengthy than the purely physical changes of puberty.

Through the process of development during adolescence, what is strived for is a sense of identity and autonomy with which to live independent lives in the world. With this the eventual aim, adolescence is often characterized by intense narcissistic preoccupations, conflict over issues of independence and major concerns about mastery and control where various skills and the adoption of a particular lifestyle is concerned (Hoffman, Becker and Gabriel 1976). Anna Freud suggests that the overarching effect of illness during adolescence is that it negates the fundamental progression toward that independent adult status understood to be the aim of this time of development. Moreover, it is Freud's assertion that 'the shedding of childish ways…can become increasingly complicated if at a time when the body…instead of being a potential symbol of pride, strength and advance, becomes a source of pain, fear and deterioration' (Freud, in Hoffman *et al.* 1976, p.xii).

A period of illness, set in the context of this view, therefore serves to threaten the self-management of bodily functions and relative freedom from the control of others now enjoyed within this age group. It also raises fears of not being able to fully participate in life or be accepted by your direct peer group and may dash very personal hopes and dreams of physical skill, achievement or becoming sexually attractive to others.

With all this in mind, it becomes clear that episodes of illness and periods of time spent in hospital during adolescence raise issues undoubtedly quite different from those experienced by children or adults. Attempting to approach the teenage patient as you would either of those other patient groups would be fundamentally wrong. Furthermore, any attempt to offer support would lead to a significant discord because unless that support is aimed at the right level, it is never going to be wholly appropriate or satisfactory. The needs of adolescents in hospital or experiencing a period of ill health require consideration in their own right and should be met by sensitive but effective management. Therefore when considering the effects of hospitalization and being ill on adolescents, the following issues are of great significance.

A place of our own

If teenagers are admitted to hospital, unless there is a specific ward for adolescent patients they could be cared for either on an adult ward or in a children's unit, depending on their age and the availability of beds at the time. Neither of these ward environments is actually suitable (Laurent 2008), for all the reasons we have previously considered. While all young people have a different point of view, some not really minding too much where they receive their care, the generally accepted view is perhaps given by David Cottrell, a professor of child and adolescent psychiatry quoted in the *Health Service Journal* (Laurent 2008), as being that children's wards with pictures of Snow White and cartoon characters can make teenagers feel unwanted while on an adult ward they may perceive – rightly or wrongly – that no one is interested in their needs. The creation of specific adolescent wards is on the increase while a significant proportion of general children's units recognize the different needs of their teenage patients and, in settings where there is neither the space, money nor patient numbers to make an entirely separate area feasible, have sought to adapt an area of the existing ward.

The notion of separate or distinct care for adolescents is by no means modern or new on the healthcare scene. In 1959, recommendations within the Platt Report stated that the differing needs of adolescents should be recognized and that the response should be separate areas of care for teenagers. The reasons why this is still, in some settings, not seen to be a priority or an area where changes – even small ones – are quite achievable vary from place to place, but may include issues around funding, space, clientele or a lack of understanding or prioritizing among staff. This lack of understanding or of seeing adolescent needs as a priority can be significantly and at times adversely affected by the continuous changes in staffing and team leadership in healthcare settings. A ward manager who recognizes a particular issue as important, for example, may later be replaced by another whose priorities differ significantly, taking the focus of the wider team in a different direction. Similarly healthcare setting can be affected by much wider issues such as the funding or prioritizing of the National Health Service as a whole. If the needs of adolescents in hospital are recognized to be an area of great need on a national scale then healthcare trusts may find themselves in possession of an influx of money to be used specifically to improve services with this slant. Such resourcing can change fairly rapidly, however, when attention is turned towards a new area of need.

A great amount of concern is given to the financing of what could become large-scale projects such as building or totally remodelling an area of a hospital to accommodate new adolescent facilities. Lansdown (1996), however, is keen to challenge this 'all-or-nothing' view of creating appropriate provision for teenage patients, urging that what is generally required – rather than an injection of cash – is a change of attitude. His suggestion is that a willingness of staff and paediatric units to cater for the needs of adolescents as their developmental stage dictates, along with the ability of staff to swiftly and easily 'cleanse the Snoopies and Lego' from an area of the ward, thus creating a space acceptable and comfortable for teenage admissions, is what is really required. The most desirable elements of such a space seem to be a consistent level of privacy, a space to go to be away from the main ward environment (a lounge, chill-out space or den, for example) for both quiet times and social contact with other similarly aged patients, the opportunity to continue contact with friends, and the ability to make choices particularly over issues such as eating and sleeping. While there is still little or no specific training for staff in the needs of adolescent patients, what also seems to be important is staff who, rather than attempting to befriend or patronize their patients, understand young people and work with them professionally in all areas of their care (Laurent 2008).

What seems to be important for adolescents in hospital is the recognition by those involved in their care that they have somehow moved away from the things central to early and even middle childhood. This recognition is best expressed perhaps not by the provision of fine new units, but in good communication. The kind of communication that means the most may be that which says 'we will do our best not to put you next to the three-year-old, whose TV blares out Postman Pat all day long, and we will try our hardest to provide you with a space to call your own'. It is easy to see that communicating well, advocating where appropriate and negotiating both for the needs and with the demands of teenage patients falls under the umbrella of the play specialist's role.

Thou shalt not assume...!

Just as with younger children, adolescents require an adequate and appropriate level of information to be given to them regarding their condition, its treatment and as far as is possibly known, the desirable outcome of that treatment. The key thing in making this statement, again as with younger children, is an appreciation and understanding of what 'adequate and appropriate' means for teenagers. It goes without saying that this understanding will need to be adapted to the needs of individual patients. However, with their training grounded in child development, play specialists will understand generally that roughly between the ages of 11 and 15 years, young people go through a period of rapidly increasing mental capacity (Lansdown 1996). Their memory skills develop and the retention of information is much increased, as is the ability to make links between collections of facts and figures. Strategic thinking – that is, the development of coping skills – independent problem solving and self-reliance are also features of this time of development.

However, this certainly does not mean that it is reasonable to expect a young person to cope alone with the enormous stress and strain of a potentially life-changing diagnosis or to put up with the anxiety of living with a chronic condition. They require as much support to make some sense of the mind-blowing challenges faced during a period of illness at this stage of their lives as would younger children. They also should receive as much help and encouragement as an adult patient would in managing that condition so that they can eventually become self-reliant and capable in their ability to cope.

One effect of being in hospital on adolescent patients is that too much is assumed about what they do or do not know. It is often assumed that this age group will have 'got over' the childish ways of younger patients and that they will therefore no longer struggle to cope with painful, stressful or frightening procedures, coping more as might an adult patient. However, in recognizing adolescence as a developmental stage – in the ways already discussed – and in accepting that being unwell and in hospital is often very stressful, it is perhaps more realistic and more fair to expect adolescent patients to show their distress at their situation in overt ways. Panic, 'playing up', a certain rigidity in the face of change or challenging authority, depression and regressive behaviour are all natural responses to stressful experiences and therefore it is not unreasonable to observe these in adolescents seen and cared for in healthcare settings.

That said, however, the developmental shift that takes place during adolescence does mean that the capacity of teenagers to cope with their experiences of being unwell can equally be quite different to that of younger children. As their thinking and information processing develops, it is true that teenage patients may be in possession of a more solid understanding of biology, for example, and the ways in which their bodies work. A greater grasp of factual knowledge is by no means to be assumed, however, nor that it is in some way helpful to their ability to cope. It is perhaps worth considering that a great many adults have a somewhat basic or vague appreciation of the inner workings of their body (Lansdown 1996). A more solid appreciation of biology does not necessarily prepare an adolescent patient for a complex diagnosis of a condition, nor does it equip him or her to adequately cope with the stress of a potentially frightening operation or procedure. Teenagers therefore require effective, consistent support and a useful amount of information to enable them to cope as well as possible. The same approach that has previously been discussed for use with children should be adopted when talking with teenagers about their condition and treatment. It is important to first find out exactly what their level of understanding is before offering anything further, and, in doing so, using their existing knowledge as a foundation upon which any additional information that needs to be given is added.

In their extensive study discussion around adolescents in hospital, Hoffman *et al.* (1976) look into the issues experienced by adolescent patients (in the context of the American healthcare system) in great detail and take the position that young people cope more effectively with the stresses faced during a period of illness by being in receipt of 'reality-based information', which aims to help them understand as accurately as possible just what will happen to them as a result of their condition and its treatment, and what to expect during their admission to hospital. It is their observation that when given appropriate information in this way, an adolescent can 'mobilize his own inner strengths and resources to allay anxiety' (p.66).

There is a further assumption that adolescents will naturally and independently volunteer any meaningful information without necessarily being prompted. This is a dangerous assumption, as it again assumes that teenage patients are capable of communicating their needs and thoughts as would an adult in a similar situation. Part of the social development during adolescence involves the acquisition of such skills, but they must not be assumed. This is why transition programmes for young people with a chronic condition take place over several years so that teenage and young adult patients can develop the ability to discuss their condition reliably and coherently with the healthcare professionals involved in their care. The acquisition of communication skills takes time and practice, especially for those in an age group notorious (according to parents at least!) for their lack of good communication. Therefore it is possibly most advisable to expect teenage patients not necessarily to volunteer information about how they are, and even when asked directly, they may not be able to express clearly how they are or any concerns or frustrations they may have.

There is also the possibility that teenagers may be afraid to voice some of their anxieties for fear of looking silly or childish. Adolescence is a time when how you are perceived and received by others takes on great importance (Lansdown and Walker 1996), therefore concerns about being seen to be weak or daft may be very real to young people, requiring the response of those caring for them to be sensitive as well as open to hearing about worries and fears, however irrational or otherwise any information offered might be.

Further to this, when considering the capacity of teenagers to cope with stressful or potentially frightening procedures, they can sometimes be one of the most challenging groups to work with. Conversely, having discussed their lack of knowledge on issues of health and illness, this may actually be because they have acquired so much of a certain type of information from the world around them and, in particular, television shows and films, some of which may be either inaccurate or extreme in their portrayal of hospitals and illness.

Popular TV shows, such as the British drama series *Casualty* or its American counterpart *ER*, may have given a sense of familiarity with a hospital environment but are frequently very graphic and also appeal to the human attraction towards the dramatic. Teenagers who are familiar with such shows, especially those who may yet have no first-hand experience of hospital treatment, on their first admission to hospital may experience extreme anxiety because their only point of reference is a TV show where every second character seems to bleed or vomit profusely before dying in a horribly noisy and tragic manner! Breaking down such points of reference, and replacing them with a more accurate and realistic set of expectations is very important in equipping teenagers for coping as well as possible with the experience of being admitted to hospital for treatment. For play specialists working in areas such as Accident and Emergency or Outpatients, or on meeting newly admitted patients, this could form an important aspect of their work.

The tendency to make assumptions about the ability and capacity of sick adolescents has the potential to be damaging in that it may lead to the needs of individual young people being cared for being significantly overlooked. To make assumptions may also place an awful lot of unrealistic expectations on young people who are unwell and therefore, rather than being more capable, are likely to be feeling somewhat vulnerable.

Dependent independence

One of the most challenging things about being ill during adolescence, it might be observed, is that at just the time in life when young people are striving and acquiring the skills needed to become more independent, their condition forces them to be dependent on others – either their parents, healthcare staff caring for them, or both. Successful separation from the nuclear family unit can be difficult enough to encourage and achieve among those who experience a relatively normal adolescence, but may present as especially challenging for those coping with a period of illness or hospitalization, and in particular for those young people who have a chronic disease or condition (Eiser 1995). The additional stresses experienced by this age group in the face of a chronic illness, such as cystic fibrosis, are gradually being more widely recognized. This is partly because more and more children with this and other long-term conditions now tend to live well into and beyond their teenage years, which was not always the case (Eiser 1995; Lansdown 1996).

The exaggerated aspects of dependence upon parents may include the practical administration of regular treatment or physiotherapy, an increase in this assistance during periods of acute illness or crises, transportation to and from hospital appointments, and communication with doctors and other healthcare professionals. If the diagnosis of a condition occurs during adolescence, for example in the case of diabetes or Crohn's (inflammatory bowel) disease – both of which have a relatively high onset during this period of development – it is quite often the case that young people may feel they have to relinquish some of their newly acquired independence in order to adapt to a new way of living with increased help from their parents. The relative loss or restriction of their independence may be the cause of much frustration, resentment or angst and may impact on their sense of self-esteem and self-belief. They may also find themselves addressing issues around their own mortality during a period of development when many young people live with a sense of invincibility. They may feel a sense of alienation from their peers (Dempsey 2008) and all this may lead to feelings of anger, depression or hopelessness.

By contrast, some young people, especially those who have lived with a chronic condition since early childhood, may struggle to take on a sense of responsibility where their own health and condition is concerned. They may be observed to have a somewhat learned sense of dependence on their parents, who may have long held a significant responsibility for the administration of their treatment. This 'learned helplessness' – of a kind – negates or may actually prevent the acquisition of skills needed in order to achieve a greater sense of independence. Family dynamics may need to be sensitively considered by the wider multidisciplinary team in such cases, as parents and their children may mutually feel this type of dependence. Addressing the history of their condition, the relationships in connection with that condition and the sense of control and purpose keenly felt by parents may be a tricky area to approach both verbally and practically with families.

Laura was 16 when she came with her mother to see the pae-diatric dermatology nurse specialist and play specialist as part of the children's dermatology clinic. She had had severe eczema since she was a baby and, after experiencing a seri-ous flare-up of the condition, came to discuss its manage-ment. During the appointment it became apparent that Laura knew little about the different medications and ointments she was using to treat her skin condition. Her mother took the lead in describing the difficulties they were facing, answering most of the questions asked, even those directed specifically at Laura herself and complaining that she and Laura frequently fell out over 'having her creams put on'. After further discus-sion, it materialized that, from the age of two, Laura had sat up on the kitchen table every morning and evening to have her creams applied by her mother. Now, at 16, they were continu-ing with the same routine, neither able to instigate a change in habit or role.

Valuable sensitive input was given by the dermatology nurse specialist, who broached with Laura's mother the sub-ject of a change in method by allowing Laura a more indepen-dent approach to managing her own treatment. Meanwhile, the play specialist worked with Laura to help her achieve a better understanding of the different functions of her various treatments, how she might go about applying them mostly by herself, though with help as required, and to increase her confidence and self-esteem by taking more responsibility for her own treatment. The extent of Laura's condition seemed to improve in the weeks that followed, and both Laura and her mother felt their relationship had also benefited somewhat from the encouragement of a more appropriate balance of roles with regard to her treatment.

The needs of siblings

Life can be tough for siblings of sick children. These brothers and sisters will almost certainly experience life in an entirely different way from most of their peers, yet may be quite unable to share or express what that experience is like with anybody. They may some-times be faced by quite overwhelming emotions yet without a readily available outlet for these strong feelings. They may spend an awful lot of time in hospitals or at appointments and may appear be knowl-edgeable beyond their years about a condition and its treatment. Yet they may well receive none of the attention that seems to be given to their sick brother or sister. Children who have sick brothers and sisters may therefore struggle with some deep, negative emotional feelings. It is also the case, however, that with appropriate support and a strong, positive family set-up many of these children can also discover depths within their sibling relationships that can go some way in overcoming these difficulties (Barrell 2004).

While the difficulties facing siblings of sick children and, to a greater or lesser extent, their needs are regularly acknowledged in literature, there are few professionals whose work is dedicated ex-clusively to supporting these children, who may be in danger of, quite literally, being 'the poor relation' in the situation facing their families. While it is usually and appropriately the case that the needs of the child who is a patient in hospital must take precedence for play specialists, it is also relatively common for them also to spend a considerable amount of time with the siblings.

Often this contact happens in the playroom, where siblings often join in with free-play activities. However, in certain circumstances, the play specialist may deliver one-to-one sessions to siblings, which may include offering preparation if their brother or sister is to un-dergo a lengthy course of treatment, for example, or one that will somehow bring about a change in their appearance or ability. In these circumstances, play specialists involved would approach chil-dren in the same way that they would their sick brothers and sisters, by assessing their cognitive development and immediate needs and planning sessions that contain something of a therapeutic bent, such as providing activities that allow children to express or face feelings of frustration and anger.

Siblings may have to spend a considerable amount of their time in the care of friends and relatives while their parents are in hospital with their sick brother or sister. This can be very stressful and unsettling for all concerned and may have the effect of making these brothers and sisters feel if not excluded then certainly quite detached from the important treatment and experiences that the sick child is having whilst in hospital and the attention he or she receives relatively exclusively from their parents during that time. They may feel equally excluded if they spend a good deal of time accompanying their brother or sister to and from hospital, doctor's appointments, therapy or treatment sessions of various kinds.

In these circumstances, there may be significant pressure on these children to 'be good' for their parents, to sit still, to amuse themselves, to wait or to be quiet. As a result, when they are in an environment where there is play provision – especially the open access environment of the ward playroom – siblings of sick children may need permission or to be given opportunities to be very physical, to be noisy, to run, jump or to smash things up. Aggressive or very physical play of this nature could involve using resources such as sand, Lego or playdough to be pummelled, built with, modelled or knocked down. It may also include building towers or models with bricks or even large soft-play blocks that can then be enthusiastically knocked over. Brothers and sisters should also be given regular access to supervised outdoor play if at all possible, so as to give them a break from the boring, stuffy and restrictive environment of the hospital ward. Noisy, boisterous and physical play of this nature has a value and significance all of its own to children whose brother or sister is ill.

It is also the case that sometimes siblings of sick children have witnessed traumatic events that may have led up to their brother or sister's admission to hospital, or they may be struggling with the details or circumstances of a child's diagnosis, condition or treatment. In some cases, the needs of a patient's siblings may be seen as taking a higher priority and the play specialist will aim to plan and work with them with a similar approach as she would have to a child who was a inpatient. Equally, just as her work would not seek to explicitly analyse or lead a child into an overt therapy-type of set-up, the play specialist may often observe and notice the themes or narratives that occur within the play in which siblings choose to engage. Should these present any cause for concern, discussion should take place with the child's parents, where necessary and appropriate, and with others within the multidisciplinary team.

Harvey was four years old when his 20-month-old brother Sam was badly scalded in an accident in the kitchen at home. Sam was cared for in hospital for nearly four weeks, during which time Harvey was a regular in the ward playroom. Harvey and Sam's mum and dad were shocked and distressed by the circumstances and severity of Sam's injury. Harvey was often sent to the playroom when they were upset, talking to the doctor or calming a distressed Sam. He took up a wide variety of free-play activities and was by no means disruptive or difficult. On one occasion, late in the afternoon, Harvey was the only child in the playroom with the play specialist who got out the Duplo building bricks and vehicles for him to play with. The play specialist also sat on the floor and played with Harvey, letting him lead the game.

As they played, they first built cars and raced them, smashing them together to end the game. Then Harvey insisted that together they build higher and higher towers which were repeatedly and enthusiastically knocked and broken down. Harvey's narrative involved police cars, ambulances, sirens and people shouting and crying and was made using an increasingly louder voice and an increasingly urgent tone. The play specialist did not attempt to guide Harvey's play, but observed this narrative with interest, knowing that Harvey had witnessed Sam's injury, and the panic that followed it at home a few weeks beforehand. At that time an ambulance had been called, Sam and his mum had been taken to the hospital and Harvey had been left at home with his grandmother who lived very locally.

This episode of playing might have been the first time that Harvey was freely able to express or re-visit some of the frightening scenes and emotions he witnessed when Sam's injury occurred. The frenetic nature of Harvey's playing eventually subsided and the free play continued at a more manageable, less intense or physical level thereafter.

The example of Harvey shows how, when siblings are regular visitors to their sick brothers and sisters, they can end up spending a lot of time in the ward playroom. If their brother or sister is an inpatient on a long-term basis or is regularly and repeatedly admitted to hospital, they might become very well known to the staff, especially the ward play staff. While this is more often than not a positive and valuable experience for all involved, siblings may sometimes become a source of concern as they can become very familiar with the hospital, the ward environment and its staff. While this can be a pleasant and positive scenario, in some cases siblings may be unsupervised for periods of time and consequently become bored, frustrated or resentful in response to the situation currently affecting their family.

Therefore when considering the overarching needs of the brothers and sisters of sick children, there seem to be two main issues that may need to be suitably addressed. If these – outlined below – are suitably addressed, a plan can be put in place to best support siblings and to aim to prevent any very negative responses they may have to the experiences affecting their family.

Communication

Just as it is possible for sick children to feel distressed or frustrated if they think that they are not being told enough about their condition or its treatment, similarly siblings can struggle if they feel excluded from important information or decisions. Because they may spend relatively prolonged periods of time away from their parents and sick sibling, this difficulty may be compounded by a sense of being excluded and/or somehow separate from the events affecting their brother, sister or family as a whole.

For this reason, the play specialist may recognize and prioritize the needs of siblings to be as great (or sometimes greater) than those of the sick child him- or herself. After discussion with parents, the play specialist may provide preparation or information sharing sessions with brothers and sisters. By this they will endeavour to try to ensure that they have been given adequate and appropriate information to encourage them to cope as well as possible.

This might be the approach of the play specialist particularly in the case of older siblings of babies or very young patients, children in intensive care or babies in special care units or whose siblings may undergo significant changes in appearance or ability following treatment for a condition. Examples of this situation might include siblings of children who may lose their hair due to a course of chemotherapy or those who may require an external fixator following leg surgery.

Recognition that siblings have their own needs

In addition to the likelihood of a lack of communication, there a particular danger lying not so much in the effects of a child's illness on his or her siblings, but in the likelihood that both the everyday and the additional needs of the siblings could go unnoticed or receive an inadequate response.

There is possibly a risk of this happening for older siblings, where there could be an expectation that they should be old enough to cope or to live relatively independent lives. This issue could equally affect siblings who are either very young at the point of their brother or sister's diagnosis or are born into a family where a child is already sick. In the case of these children, there can be an assumption that they don't know any different or – if they are still relatively young – would not necessarily understand the issues affecting their family.

By their ability to observe children's behaviour and assess their individual needs, play specialists involved in caring for sick children, in also getting to know their siblings, will recognize that they have significant needs and that they may still feel anxiety or resentment at the situation affecting their family. Provision in response to these needs may be very similar to that given to the sick child him- or herself. Play specialists may also aim to support families as well as possible by planning set times for play sessions with the child who is sick, specifically so that parents can have regular time to spend with their well children. Knowing that their sick child will benefit from the input of the play specialist can help parents to feel confident leaving them so that they can also set time aside to spend with their other children.

Further support

Where there is concern for the needs of the families of sick children, any observations or thoughts can often be brought to and shared within multidisciplinary team meetings. These concerns may well be either for the wellbeing of siblings or down to any problems caused by their difficult behaviour within the ward environment. How best to support the whole family should be a multidisciplinary team decision, although specific support offered may include referring brothers or sisters to a local sibling support or young carers' group, or if these options are not readily available, making a referral to a Local Authority Family Support team. While such services can be invaluable to families of sick children, if referring children to an independent or external group, it is important to avoid giving them the impression that they are a problem that needs fixing or, in effect, causing them to feel further excluded from the family group, especially if they have already struggled with this. If there are significant concerns about a family by the multidisciplinary team, a referral may be made to a clinical psychologist or the local Child and Adolescent Mental Health Service (CAMHS) for further support or family therapy.

In conclusion then, during a time of being sick or in hospital and its related stress and strain, children of the four distinct age groups considered in this chapter clearly face many differing issues. Some of these issues will be different purely because they are specific or are felt especially keenly by children during a particular life stage. However, while recognizing and respecting this, there are also significant aspects of this experience that are similar regardless of age or life stage. Overall there are two broad similarities that remain throughout the course of childhood and these should perhaps underpin the approach of the play specialist in working with sick children and young people.

The first of these is that regardless of the child's age or ability a period of illness and particularly of hospitalization brings with it the potential for his or her development to be delayed or behaviour and sense of emotional wellbeing to be affected adversely. The second is the tendency to make assumptions about children's knowledge and understanding. These assumptions are made, first, about the level of knowledge that children already have – usually a judgement made based upon an understanding of age or developmental stage in relation to children's abilities. There is also a tendency to assume that children will not cope if they are given 'too much' information about their condition or its treatment. The difficulty with making assumptions about what children know, understand or should be told is that doing so fails to recognize the differing needs and abilities of individual children regardless of their differing ages and stages.

How might the play specialist's approach reflect an acceptance of these issues? What place does play have for sick children and young people?

In considering both of these broad issues that may significantly affect children and young people in hospital, a conclusion can be drawn highlighting the need to recognize that all children irrespective of their age face the possibility of risk where the continuation of their development is concerned. Equally, within the involvement of the play specialist in the care of sick children, he or she should look to avoid making assumptions about what children already know or how they may be inclined to react when receiving sensitive, complex or distressing information. Therefore the need to assess – either instinctively, based on knowledge, training and extensive experience or explicitly by the use of a tool or particular set of questions/criteria – and to base any work on the specific needs of individual patients should be regarded as key to this approach.

The play specialist's aim should be to offer appropriate information and effective emotional support, alongside the basic provision of normalizing play facilities, all of which should be planned according to the needs of each individual child. Undoubtedly much of the play specialist's work will be similar for children at certain ages. Our earlier acceptance that there is a commonly held understanding of what is normal and expected of children throughout childhood informs this. However, this must not allow all children to be simply lumped together, since this would fail both to identify the needs of individual children and to offer them an appropriate and adequate level of support in a time that can be strange, stressful and sometimes traumatic.

The play specialist's role is also significant in that it potentially serves to bridge the communication that happens between sick children and those people who are involved in their care. When supporting children, particularly but not exclusively those who are in hospital, the play specialist specifically aims to assist children and young people in making sense of their experiences while they are ill. They can also communicate a child's needs and reactions to his or her illness and treatment to the wider multidisciplinary team. Further still, the play specialist can also be effective in informing on and discussing with parents and carers the journey they may take through the treatment upon which they embark as a family and what they might expect for and from their child who is unwell.

In an article entitled 'A plea for play', Peg Belson made just that: a plea for more play in hospitals. Here the statement was made that 'if the hospital is to care for the whole child, physically, mentally and emotionally, it must provide suitable play facilities supervised by a trained member of staff as an integral part of the [child's] treatment plan' (Belson 1987, p.16). Within a range of healthcare environments, where children can run the risk of being defined or referred to only in terms of their physical condition, the approach of the play specialist is a holistic one – that is, concerned with the needs of the whole child, not just his or her physical state.

Having established the distinct role of the play specialist and having considered the effects of a period of illness or hospitalization might have on the wellbeing of children and young people, the chapters that follow will look in greater detail at the three main aspects of the play specialist's role in working with sick children and young people.

4

More than Just Playing: The Importance of Normalizing Play

When a child is in hospital he is in danger of losing contact with the outside world, which has been up to that time the background of his development. (Platt 1959, p.18)

As one of the key tenets of the play specialist's work, the provision of 'normalizing play' arguably constitutes the grass roots upon which the more specialized areas of practice are based. Giving sick children access to familiar, straightforward play activities was the aim of the first play leaders, most of them volunteers, in hospital settings. The scope of the play specialist's role has grown and expanded over time, and indeed continues in so doing. Recognition that sick children still need to have access to familiar play activities and appropriate provision in response to this need remains a key element to the role and work of play specialists.

To gain something of a clearer understanding of the function of normalizing play for sick children and young people it is first important to consider what we know and understand about play and then to define or describe or what needs to be understood by the term 'normalizing'.

What is meant and understood by 'play'?

There have been a great many attempts to define play or to pin down the very nature or function of playful activities, yet most of those who write on play are agreed, at the very least, on one thing and that is that to produce a concise definition of why children play is virtually impossible (Meadows 1986; Smith, Cowie and Blades 2003).

'And why not?' one could ask.

It actually seems wholly appropriate that a cover-all explanation for why children play is hard to find. That we can establish no hard and fast explanation or definition of play seems very fitting. Immense and profound in its place in a child's life and development, the purpose of play is clearly complex and yet its activities can appear so simple, occurring most naturally and seemingly with the minimal amount of adult influence. Since play is a freely flowing activity, naturally undertaken and almost always driven by children, to put 'what play is' in a box would somehow diminish from the vitality, adaptability, complexity and value of play for children in all areas of their development and at all ages. Accepting then that it is hard to find a precise and absolute definition of what play is, it is valuable to consider that which is known, generally understood and agreed upon where play is concerned.

Play is universally regarded as being the predominant occupation of children, and furthermore over time has increasingly been recognized as being an essential part of a healthy childhood (Weller 1980; Lansdown and Walker 1996). Theories of play have changed and developed over time but have considered play to be multi faceted in its function for children, relevant and contributory to all areas of their development.

As long ago as the age of ancient Greek philosophy, first Plato (427–347 BC) and later Aristotle (384–322 BC) recognized the practical value of play in the facilitation of skills and conceptual learning in children. Since the late nineteenth century, the purpose of play has been a significant part of the discussion around how children grow and learn. This discussion has provided an arena within which there has been much debate and disagreement, as well as bringing forth some significant insights into the world and work of children.

Herbert Spencer, professor of psychology and author of *The Principles of Psychology* (1898), gave the view that play was simply a means by which children could work off excess energy. This, however, was a view criticized by his contemporary Karl Groos who looked both at the play behaviours of animals (1898) as well as people (1901). Groos, by contrast, viewed play as having a far more definite function, seeing it as useful in terms of the acquisition of skills required to find a role in adult life. His view held that play provided the practice and elaboration of skills necessary for survival, stating that 'perhaps the very existence of youth is largely for the sake of play' (Smith *et al.* 2003, p.193). This theory of play as being for the acquisition and practice of life skills echoes still in many modern views of play. It was by no means taken as the definitive explanation for why children play, however, and did meet with some opposition, particularly by G. Stanley Hall – a further contemporary of Groos and Spencer – who instead postulated that rather than being a means of preparation for future roles and skills, play was more a recapitulation of man's primitive past. Cathartic in nature, according to Hall, play allowed for the 'playing out' of characteristics or instincts found in earlier human history (Smith *et al.* 2003, p.193).

Further hypothesizing over the function of play grew and gathered momentum throughout the early to mid-twentieth century. Theorists from the schools of developmental psychology, psychoanalysis, evolutionary theory and education philosophy were among those all contributing ideas to a melting pot. Of note were Sigmund

Freud (1856–1939) and later his daughter Anna (1895–1982) who, as psychoanalysts, viewed play as 'an unconscious expression of a painful memory or desire or a re-enactment of a pleasant experience' (Lansdown 1996, p.64). The Freuds were key figures in the development of the play therapy movement, which seeks to understand children's experiences by interpreting their responses and behaviour in play, and which, in turn, influenced the development of the provision of play for children in hospital.

Arguably one of the most influential theorists where play is concerned was Jean Piaget (1896–1980) whose stage-related hypothesis became the accepted view of how children develop through play for much of the last century and significantly influenced the training of childcare practitioners, especially those involved in education. For Piaget, play was purely about assimilation – that is to say, the receiving and understanding – of information from the world around the child. Play was the means by which children could make sense of the world, but in order to do so four distinct stages were to be worked through and these began and ended at fairly standard, age-related periods of childhood. To develop fully in all areas, children merely travelled through these stages, playing in a particular way at a given age after which they moved on to the next stage and so on.

Piaget's stages, in the briefest sense, consisted first of practice play – known as the 'sensory motor' stage – occurring between birth and two years. This was followed between two and seven years by the 'pre-operational' stage of make-believe or symbolic play. Next came a period of rule-bound play from the age of seven to around 12 years – the 'concrete operational' stage, and finally children's development was complete by the age of 18 once the child had mastered the area and stage of 'abstract thought' and play.

For some time Piaget's theory was widely regarded as indisputable – a 'fait accompli' in terms of understanding children's development and within it the place of play. In the latter half of the twentieth century, however, Piaget's views began to become the subject of increasing challenge. The main aspect of the stage-related theory of play to have been disputed is that it provides too rigid a view of children's development and does not recognize the development of each individual child at a unique pace, by treading his or her own path towards new developmental milestones. Piaget felt that children could only move forward into the next stage and that back stepping or re-visiting an area for a period of time was simply not possible. The result of the challenge to Piaget's theories is that while still respected, most developmental psychologists and academics no longer accept them as a wholly accurate description of how children play and develop. It is clear that children's play does tend to follow some recognizable patterns as they move through their development and therefore while Piaget's theories have rightly been challenged, it would still be unwise to discredit or write them off completely.

The discovery of the work of Russian academic Lev Vygotsky (1896–1934) offered some of the most direct challenges to Piaget's theories. A direct contemporary of Piaget, Vygotsky died young, while Piagetian theory was still largely taken as read by Western countries, and his work and thoughts on play were not released outside Russia until their translation into English in the 1960s and 1970s. There was clear disparity between the work of Piaget and that of Vygotsky who saw real value in the imaginary elements of children's play. Rather than fantasy and pretend play being merely a stage to be worked through – a restrictive box within which certain skills and abilities were honed before proceeding to the stage that followed – it was seen as a way that children could step outside the restrictions of real life and freely explore meaning (Lindon 2001). For Vygotsky also, play had a significant place in the process of learning but it was not the only way that children learned and he was keen that the focus should not always fall on the intellectual gains achievable through play. Vygotsky stressed that the emotional exploration made possible by play was also of great important to the child.

The issue of the contribution of play to children's emotional health and wellbeing has become a key feature of more modern thinking on the value of play for children and young people. Greater attention has been paid to the importance of the play spaces children inhabit (Hughes 2001), and how the size, contents and condition of these can influence the desire and ability of children to access and use such facilities. There has also been a move to understand the influence of adults on children's play and the importance of freedom in play to make discoveries, try out new skills, take risks or make independent choices.

The value of such play can be observed even in the very youngest children, particularly, for example, in the encouragement of heuristic play for babies. In something of a move away from play facilities which are designed by adults for use by children and tend to involve either a very limited or very specific way of playing, with the purpose of achieving a set and specific outcome, the approach of heuristic play, as devised and described by Elinor Goldschmied, encourages 'spontaneous exploratory activity' with natural objects and artefacts that are not traditionally recognizable as play things. With these, children can play freely and imaginatively, at their own pace and using all of their senses to make discoveries about the world around them (Goldschmied and Jackson 2004).

Given that much play theory has for so long been linked to education and children's assimilation of new skills and information, modern thought on play has shifted the focus towards a more psychosocial stance. Bob Hughes, Fraser Brown and Brian Sutton-Smith are key figures in discussing the effects of play on brain, conduct and social development and long-term behavioural issues. They highlight the harmful effects of so-called play deprivation, which makes for very interesting reading when set against the social climate in the UK today. Here, youth culture is often regarded as something to be feared and where threats or actual acts of violence and aggression are regularly carried out by or against young people themselves. Gang culture, knife and gun crimes, yob behaviour and a lack of respect for other citizens would seem to be increasingly prevalent and certainly so if the tabloid press are to be taken at their word.

Sutton-Smith (1997) questions what the effects might be for children if they do not get adequate or appropriate opportunities to play. His suggestion is that an outcome of being chronically deprived of play would be the impairment of behaviour or conduct because the role of play is specifically to do with the 'actualisation of brain potential' (cited by Hughes in Brown 2003, p.73). He describes in detail the make-up of the human brain from birth, and suggests that play is the key to healthy and optimal brain development which later makes possible appropriate brain processes and appropriate responses socially and personally. That the importance of play is discussed in such scientific terms and recognized as being so central to human development represents a significant move forward in giving play the value and respect it is due. Play is increasingly recognized as being more than an assistant or even a foundation to children's education, or just something that is simply lovely and fun to do. Play is no longer understood to be merely the means by which children make sense of the world. Moreover it is perhaps the very means by which they are able to successfully, appropriately and wholly discover and take up their place within it. Play is increasingly being recognized as having a fundamental role in what it means to be human and being essential to healthy, complete development, particularly where social, emotional, behavioural and empathetic abilities are concerned.

What is clear from this discussion, then, is that play is difficult to define in simple terms, but is unequivocally central to children's development. It seems that it is neither possible nor advisable simply to view play merely from one single theoretical standpoint. What would perhaps be more valuable would be to aim for a view that incorporates varied aspects of the play theories outlined above.

Play is accepted as being a significant means by which children learn about, experiment and connect with the world around them. It provides a functional means to the acquisition of many of the skills – practical, social and cognitive – required to function within society. It is also primarily a pleasurable experience, though one through which children can express and attempt to make sense of the stress and trauma that childhood can bring. From this they significantly and undoubtedly benefit on an emotional, psychological and social level. Play provides the building blocks to independence and successful functioning within the world, but it is not merely a means to an end – its value is just as great in the here and now of children's everyday play experiences as it is in terms of storing up knowledge and understanding useful to the child's future.

What is meant and understood by the term 'normalizing'?

The use of the term 'normalizing' assumes a scenario that is somehow abnormal and in need of transformation to something more familiar, manageable and altogether more normal, but what is it that we understand to be meant by the expression 'normal' for today's children?

The use of the term 'normal' is often met with controversy, but nonetheless it is often used by those working with, observing and describing the behaviour or ability of children. Its use serves to express something of a commonly held understanding of the experiences of a majority of children and families. While it is neither sensible nor realistic to imagine that all children share and enjoy a childhood that is happy, carefree or privileged, in seeking to define what is normal in any given context, it is valuable to gain awareness that a definition of 'normal' – or otherwise – will always be based upon both a set of expectations and also a collection of pre-judgements.

When thinking specifically about children, there is certainly a spectrum of expectations or understanding around various aspects of children's lives – a wide middle ground between narrower extremes. The common experiences of the majority of children, as previously discussed, fall into this wide middle ground and are therefore generally understood and accepted as being 'the norm'. When considering the case of sick children, significant expectations tend to be concerned with the ability or level of understanding of an individual or a particular group as defined by age or gender for example. A knowledge of child development – based in itself on observations of 'normal' milestones across a large number of children studied over time – allows us to conclude, for example, that certain behaviour is normal or otherwise when observed in a child by the time he or she reaches a certain age.

However, making assumptions about what children and young people know and understand carries the danger of approaching a situation with a set of expectations already in place, which may prevent the needs of children as individuals being sought, identified and appropriately met.

The pre-judgements with which any work with children and families may be approached is an even more precarious area, since the desire to define things, people, situations or behaviours as being normal (or otherwise) is largely based on whether they are somehow acceptable or not, on a social, cultural or personal basis. This view of normality is very subjective, and is frequently influenced by various factors that differ from individual to individual, such as culture, race, religion, gender, chosen lifestyle and life experiences.

The theoretical issues encountered when considering what is meant or understood as something 'being normal', or otherwise, are clearly fraught with difficulty. While in a number of contexts there is certain agreement around the wide middle ground that exists and into which the experience of most children falls, there is simultaneously an acceptance that every aspect of every child's life experience is different in various ways to that of his or her peers, even subtly so. What is normal for one family or individual will be different to what is accepted as normal for others.

Perhaps when considering what is meant by normal, the question thrown straight back should be: 'Whose normal are we talking about?' The issue of normality becomes contentious when you consider that normal, far from being the same, is in fact different for every child! When planning for and reflecting on good practice with children and young people, then, it is important for play specialists to consider some of the assumptions that can easily be made about children, families and play in today's society (because a view of what is normal is always a construction, a set of ideas, bound by the current values and expectations of a given society (Jenks 1996)). For example, is it largely assumed that it is normal for children to play and play regularly? Is the expectation that the home is the place where children do most of their playing? Is it imagined that for most children, home is a place of comfort and emotional security rather than a place of anxiety, stress or trauma?

The child of today...?

The child of today is better housed, better clothed, and better nourished than at any time in our history. His individuality is recognised and appreciated both at home and in school and there is a growing readiness to understand and care for his emotional needs. (Platt 1959, p.2)

In 1959, the general introduction to the Platt Report contained this statement, so general as to be sweeping, which referred to changes that had taken place in the lives of children. These changes were understood to be so profound that they necessitated a major change at all levels in the approach to their healthcare, and particularly their care when in hospital. As the effects of widespread post-war social and cultural change on children and families were recognized, so different views of childhood and children's normal life experiences were born.

While the Platt Report may have made sweeping statements or assumptions about children's lives, just as is still so often done today, it remains significant because it was one of the first voices to be heard announcing that children in the healthcare system in the UK needed to be not only viewed differently to adults, but also treated differently to them. The Platt Report, alongside the work of James and Joyce Robertson, was also one of the first significant documents to express recognition that the hospital environment was an abnormal space for children and had the potential to affect their overall state of wellbeing.

It is acknowledged, therefore, that the issue of understanding normality is, at the very least, a complex and contentious one, based upon assumptions and expectations that are societally specific. When considering normalizing play as a major part of the work provided for sick children, instead of becoming preoccupied by what is meant or understood by the term 'normalizing', it is perhaps more useful to ask what it is about their experience that we are aiming to normalize.

Bridging the gap

Maybe then, the matter of greater importance here is less about political correctness and more to do with the hospital environment being an abnormal environment in which children find themselves, which is undoubtedly very different from the familiarity of home. Perhaps it is important to worry less about the issue of whose idea of normal is more relevant or acceptable, and to move more towards a straightforward acceptance that hospitals (and other healthcare settings) are an abnormal and strange environment within which children find themselves and where they therefore need assistance to understand and cope with all that they encounter while they are there.

Healthcare settings, and hospitals in particular, are unfamiliar environments for the majority of children. They are frequently places where children experience new people, and strange or unpleasant sights, smells, noises and additional stressors that can be difficult to understand and can be traumatic. By providing and facilitating play activities, particularly in a hospital setting, play specialists can aim to support children's normal development, and so assist them in reaching their key developmental milestones. Furthermore however, play specialists recognize that play is of great value to children who are unwell because it acts as an outlet for the expression of anxiety or worry (Harvey and Hales-Tooke 1972; Weller 1980; Jolly 1981; Lansdown 1996), because it is a means for social interaction with other children, and also because it serves to bridge the gap between what a child is familiar with – those things which serve to enhance his or her sense of security and safety – and all that is unfamiliar about the experience of being ill, receiving treatment and possibly being in hospital.

The presence of play in that environment serves to act as a buffer, which allows children to gain new coping skills and take on new information. Children are also allowed to explore, encounter and make sense of the abnormality or the newness with which they are presented by being ill and in hospital. With the provision of familiar and open access play activities, the play specialist aims to normalize the sometimes bewildering, sometimes stressful and sometimes unpleasant aspects of the medical world.

More than 'just playing'

When we specifically consider children in hospital, we should not only acknowledge the importance of play as being central to and supportive of children's normal development. Since we know that without play, a child's ability to develop and function effectively in the world is at best impaired and at worst as good as impossible, when children are unwell and are perhaps required to be cared for in hospital, play should also be accepted as being crucial to their all-round wellbeing. Sheridan (1977) asserts that children in hospital have a 'very special need' for playthings and playmates. Harvey and Hales-Tooke (1972) take this statement further, emphasizing the central importance of play for children by observing that 'deprived of play the child is a prisoner, shut off from all that makes life real and meaningful' (p.23).

Therefore, it could be suggested that a major purpose for which play specialists provide and facilitate normalizing play for children in hospital, hospices, health centres or in their own homes is at least in part because it acts as a form of 'damage limitation'. That is to say, that by the provision of play for sick children, the play specialist is aiming to safeguard, as far as possible, their optimal emotional wellbeing and the continuation of normal development for each individual child with whom he or she works. Equally the play specialist is aiming to facilitate the best possible coping strategies and emotional wellbeing for the potentially stressful situation posed by a period of ill health with possible hospitalization. Although a great many approaches are employed in response to the needs of the individual child, the provision of normal, familiar play activities has a particular value to children, particularly those in hospital. Such provision sends out a powerful cue that this is a place where you can participate in familiar and therefore comforting play activities and where a sense of safety and security can be experienced.

What is play like for children?

Having considered the role and function of play in the course of a child's developmental journey, and the importance of play in seeking to normalize some of the harmful or stressful aspects of hospitalization for children, this is perhaps an appropriate time to consider what playing might actually be like for children themselves. For those who study play, or observe children at play for a significant part of their work, there is a risk of getting caught up in the theoretical or developmental aspects of why and how children play. What might sometimes get caught up in this risk is the danger of losing a sense of what playing is actually like for children. What is it like to play? What is like to get completely lost in a make-believe game? What is it like to run and jump and imagine you can fly? Adults, more often than not, have forgotten the impact of play on the senses, yet when planning and providing play activities for children, it important to consider, as well as the needs of those children for whom that play is intended, what their experience of playing might be like.

Therefore, in spite of all that is theoretically known by adults about it, for children, first and foremost, play is fun. Play provides a place to safely experiment with the acquisition of new skills, the complexity of relationships, taking risks, and thinking about complicated ideas. Children love to run, jump, spin, skip, tumble, climb and hide, using their whole bodies in play. They like to sit quietly and conscientiously concentrate on intricate craft or building tasks. They feel proud when completing a complicated model made of Lego or clay, although may also feel great excitement at building a tall tower of bricks and knocking it down with a resounding crash. They like to paint to produce a recognizable picture or simply to experiment with shape, colour, texture or technique. They like to consider the roles and experiences they have had themselves and those of other people through pretend play, and they love to immerse themselves deeply in becoming someone else in a way that is only achievable through intense fantasy play. They enjoy controlling characters and stories through using small figures or puppets and may also love the thrill of winning a word play or guessing game. They like to make a mess! They might use many toys and pieces of everyday furniture or equipment, or use nothing but their imagination and a germ of an idea. Play is exciting, it is exhilarating, challenging, and children derive great pleasure by taking part in it.

Play is often discussed or described as a singular idea, as if 'play' involves a single type of activity. However play is clearly a vast area and one that is possibly even infinite in terms of how children engage in play, the types of thought and practical activity this involves, and the different outcomes these might produce.

What do different types of play mean for children and young people?

In 1996, Bob Hughes – a theoretical and applied playworker and a major force in today's discussions and definitions of play – produced a document called *A Playworker's Taxonomy of Play Types*. In this he explains and highlights the richness and variety of play experiences for children (Lindon 2001), by outlining the following 15 different types of play. All of these, according to Hughes, are essential for children in enabling their ability to learn and develop (Hughes 2001).

Bob Hughes' definition of 'Play Types' (1996):

- symbolic play

- rough and tumble play

- socio-dramatic play

- social play

- creative play

- communication play

- exploratory play

- fantasy play

- imaginative play
- locomotor play
- mastery play
- object play
- role play
- deep play
- dramatic play.

This list of play types has formed the foundation of much discussion about play in recent years. It has been used widely by many play providers as a tool in order to create a meaningful framework of practice by which the assessment and planning of the variety of play opportunities on offer to children in specific play settings is made possible. It is however quite theoretical in its approach or viewpoint of play, and does not necessarily lend itself easily or straightforwardly to identifying the areas where children's everyday play experiences should most obviously fit.

A less theoretical and more practical application of how to define the categories of play within which children most commonly engage may perhaps be helpful in order to better understand how children might benefit from different types of play. The following descriptions of different types of play explore and discuss these more anecdotally. This, it is hoped, will produce a greater awareness of the purpose, outcomes and potential benefits to be found in the practical play activities most often chosen by children.

> ◉ *Pretend or fantasy play – 'Who will I be today?'*: This type of play allows for the exploration of specific experiences and also of more general roles, behaviour and relationships. It can provide children with a renewed sense of control

over situations that are either impossible in real life (flying or having superpowers, for example) or that are difficult to understand or cope with in reality. Pretend play, alone or with others, is the means by which children may be often found to 'play through' experiences and situations that they have witnessed or thought about. It is generally accepted that by being encouraged, helped or at least allowed to 'act it out', children can be helped to better understand aspects of life that may be painful, stressful or confusing. The value of this type of play is therefore particularly pertinent to sick children, especially if they have been hospitalized or undergone invasive treatment for a period of time.

○ *'Small world' play*: This example of play, using small models (such as dinosaurs, animals or character figures, possibly branded versions including Playmobil, Happy Land, Barbie, Action Man, Polly Pocket and Little People), has similar benefits or outcomes to those associated with pretend or fantasy play. In small world play, children can experiment with themes relating to mastery and control and can provide an arena for experimenting with ordering and exploring roles. Children may spend a large amount of time in painstakingly setting up a doll's house or animal scene, possibly narrating what they are doing all the while. This not only may allow them to address life's difficult or complex issues, but may also specifically allow them to regain a sense of control in relation to situations where they feel powerless or somehow out of control. N.B. While working with sick children, play specialists may observe recurring themes within children's play and may note these down for reference. However, analysis of such observations is not generally within the remit of their role.)

○ *Construction play*: Children may use a variety of playthings with which to build or create models, scenes, characters or contraptions including wooden bricks, blocks and train track, or brands such as Lego, Duplo, Meccano and Octons. Generally smaller in scale than junk modelling, for example (see Art and craft, below), construction play involves finely honed fine motor skills to be able to handle and manipulate various objects in order to turn imagined concepts into real models.

○ *Physical play:* This type of play can often be incorporated into many other aspects of children's play activities. They may engage in complex pretend games that also include lots of big movements or which use the large-scale pieces of physical play equipment that are often found in gardens and play areas alike. They may, for example, pretend to be a story character that flies or will use large movements in their play to act out a scene. Running, jumping, climbing, rolling, throwing and catching and using tools to hit balls or targets all provide an outlet for excessive energy, but also encourage children to learn the limits of what their body can do. Large-scale physical play allows children a sense of freedom that may not be found in any other area of play. For children who are ill or in hospital, especially if they are significantly restricted by their illness, physical play is of great importance as it not only helps to maintain and progress an area of development that may otherwise be significantly impaired, but can provide a controlled way of expressing or releasing pent-up anger, frustration or anxiety.

○ *Games with rules:* This was one of the three main areas of play discussed by Jean Piaget, who mapped its starting point at around six or seven years of age. His view was that games with rules depended upon older children gaining an understanding of abstract ideas and the concept of a certain rule or set of rules being understood, and that that understanding was equally shared with other children (Lindon 2001). Games with rules include many different types of play activities from physical games that may involve elements of fantasy or storytelling to card games, board games, games 'on paper' (noughts and crosses, or boxes, for example) and verbal games like 'I spy'.

Anecdotal observations show that it is possible for children as young as three to join in with or be taught basic versions of rule-bound games, which suggest that Piaget's age/stage theory of the development of play was not entirely accurate. He was, however, right in stating that this type of play had an important place in social development, since it involves learning about turn-taking, strategic thinking, experiencing what it is like to win and lose, learning to set – and stick to – rules, making up the rules of play, cooperation with others in this task and ultimately learning to face the consequences of breaking rules.

- *Word and number play:* This could be seen as a more specific extension of the games with rules described above which includes examples such as card games, language and word games, crosswords and word searches, riddles and joke-telling. By the nature of these types of activities being largely an extension of a taught understanding of language, spelling or maths skills, these may indeed begin to emerge amongst children from around the age of six or seven, as Piaget described. Such activities allow children to experiment and play with language or numbers. They also encourage the consolidation and application of skills learned through formal education.

- *Art and craft:* Children almost all love to engage at some level in art activities. Painting and colouring are the mainstay of many children's settings, including hospital playrooms, and not only provide a relaxing, enjoyable and flexible pastime, but can also be the means by which children can express their feelings and emotional responses to their experiences. Art and craft projects can also be one way of building a child's self-esteem since within these activities a goal can be set and achieved in a fairly straightforward way. A child may wish to draw, paint or junk model a particular thing, or try a specific craft project (weaving, friendship bracelets, clay, candle making, painting a mug, plate or tile, or creating a mosaic, for example). With some involvement from a willing adult, usually to get them started, such a plan can easily be accomplished, giving children a genuine sense of achievement.

For children in hospital, the value of art and craft play is greater still for two main reasons. First, painting (and other similar art activities, such as colouring and drawing) is a highly expressive, involuntary means of communication, through which children will present facts that surprise and enlighten the adults who care for them (Azarnoff 1986). This will either be through the images they choose to project or present through their artwork, or through the narrative that may accompany the process of such an activity. The other way that art and craft has value for children when they are unwell is not only that it can boost their self-esteem, but furthermore it can reassure them that their bodies, though ill and struggling in the present, still work and can be used for pleasure.

○ *Messy play:* The idea of 'messiness' holds certain negative connotations, particularly that it is, to a greater or lesser extent, chaotic in a world that likes order and that to create a mess is not a good thing because, for example, it is dirty, inconvenient or needs to be tidied away, which takes a further degree of effort. Messy play activities however, including those using water, shaving foam, sand, dried lentils or rice, play dough, 'gloop' (a mixture of cornflour and water) and foodstuffs such as jelly or cooked pasta are of significant value because through them children make discoveries and can be creative in an infinite number of ways.

Duffy (2007), writing for the Early Years Foundation Stage, discusses the problem of seeing messy place as chaotic or inconvenient, preferring to view this type of play as important *because* it lacks the focus on specifically making or producing something. In messy play, children are free to explore all sorts of possibilities, using all of their senses, tapping into their innate curiosity about the world and their strong desire to explore or find out more about it.

In a similar way to certain aspects of physical play and art and craft activities, messy play has particular value to children who are unwell and in hospital since it can provide an outlet for frustration, or a means to explore new or complicated ideas and situations. Messy play activities can fairly easily be brought to a child whether he or she is restricted to being in bed or otherwise. The unstructured nature of messy play can also provide welcome relief from the structure of the hospital environment and treatment regimes.

○ *Risky play:* This area of play is possibly the one that is least often catered for, either by choice or by circumstance in children's services. It is, in itself, a slightly controversial area, probably because Western culture is one that currently doesn't like to present children with risks, since these involve the possibility (real or imagined) of injury, catastrophe or litigation. However, it is becoming recognized anew that such play activities as using tools, lighting fires, climbing, den building, playing up high and squeezing into tight spaces do have great value to children's development in a number of areas. Risky play encourages children to find the limits to their strength and abilities – running, jumping, lifting; it allows children and young people to gain skills in personal risk assessment – what is too high, too small, too complicated, too vulnerable when on your own; on seeking thrills and realizing achievements – a successful leap, a den that stays up, a height reached. All get the heart racing, the blood pumping and the brain thinking and problem solving.

⬤ *Outdoor play – 'A breath of fresh air':* In a similar way to risky play, outdoor play is an area that, in the last generation, has seen significant changes. Until a generation ago, it was very common for most children to play outside on a very regular basis, individually or in groups, roaming freely or engaged in some form of organized play activities. Society today has experienced shifts in parenting styles and media influence, which along with some other factors have made it significantly less common for children to play outside the confines of their own home and garden. Increased parental worries about the safety of their children and a desire therefore to keep them close to home or within the home for the majority of their non-school time is an important issue contributing to this change as is a significant increase in children's dependence on television programmes and computer games for entertainment (Clements 2004).

In an age where there are increased concerns about the state of children's physical health and poor social skills, the reduction in children taking part in outdoor play activities is becoming a cause for concern, in spite of the benefits of playing outside being widely recognized. This was highlighted through research undertaken by Barnardo's which showed that 83 per cent of parents surveyed saw outdoor play as desirable or important for their children yet only 13 per cent of children regularly played freely out of doors (Barnardo's and Transport 2000 Association of London Government 2004).

Children's development is helped significantly by outdoor play, particularly in terms of their physical development. Research has highlighted a wide range of benefits of active play including how it stimulates the child's digestive system, helping to improve appetite, which in turn acts to ensure continued strength and bodily growth (Clements

1998; Pica 2003, discussed in Clements 2004), plus the positive effects that outdoor physical play can have on the growth of a child's muscles, heart and lungs as well as other vital organs.

When considering the issue of outdoor play, if it is at all possible for an outdoor space to be provided for children in hospital the value of such provision should not be underestimated. Hospital wards can prove to be noisy, stuffy, hot, cluttered, sometimes smelly places where a child or family's sense of personal space can be heavily impeded. Finding a play area where there is fresh air, space, different play activities and within which greater physical activity can be positively encouraged is often possible, and should be acknowledged to be hugely important to sick children, especially those who may have been in hospital for some time. A sense of becoming somewhat institutionalized – that is a sense of being confined (*Collins English Dictionary* 1999) or removed from the world outside – can set in fairly easily and after only a relatively short time. It is important and significant for children in this position to be able to spend time in the relative space and freedom that can be found outside and to re-engage in the world and wider society outside of the hospital environment.

The 'duality' in normalizing play for sick children

With their knowledge of child development and the effects of being unwell on children, and a theoretical understanding of the functions of play, an important skill of the play specialist is clearly to recognize that there is something of a duality in the nature of normalizing play provided for sick children. Play activities as experienced by children exist because they are fun, exciting, stimulating and allow for busyness, exploration and pure, simple pleasure. The duality of such activities exists by the play specialist's recognition that far from being 'just playing' – as many children will report when asked how they have spent their time – they are hugely value-laden.

For children in hospital there is the added value that play does have a therapeutic role in aiding children in their ability to cope with stress and process information, and in its attempts to normalize the strangeness of their experience. Never trivial, the provision of familiar, comforting and arguably normal play activities for children in hospital should be regarded as fundamentally central to the care given and the support offered to them.

How do play specialists use normalizing play?

As has been demonstrated, play specialists use normalizing play in a great variety of ways. The play provision offered may very well be tailored in response to the needs of patients on an individual basis and in such cases may be delivered on a one-to-one basis. By comparison, general play is often also set up and overseen for a large number of children who can freely access the activities provided at the same time, in a waiting area or ward playroom. Within some larger play departments, normalizing play activities in a communal area, and sometimes one-to-one play sessions at a child's bedside, might be provided by a play assistant under the guidance of a play specialist within the wider team.

Play specialists work in highly varied settings and the needs of the children with whom they work are constantly changing. They are therefore required to consider many factors in planning and prioritizing the service they provide. Depending upon the nature of these different factors, the style of working may vary considerably. With this in mind it is worth accepting that no one method of working is right or wrong, but rather the key to good practice is in being able to organize the work that is needed, to deliver the best possible provision for those children that need it at any given time, using the most appropriate and useful resources available.

Table 4.1 Exploring the duality of normalizing play for sick children

Type of normalizing play activity offered	Age suitability	Supports area of development	Experienced as important by the child in the following ways	Recognized as valuable in other ways specific to children in hospital
Home corner	18 months +	Cognitive; social; understanding of roles, routines, etc.	Fun!; pretend play and exploration of the world	Allows children to re-visit the rules, routines, objects and other features of home that are familiar, comforting and 'normal'
Playdough	1 year +	Fine motor skills; cognitive/ imagination	Fun!; tactile; new textures explored; imagination can be utilized	Can allow for the release of pent-up anxiety or frustration; tactile working of dough is relaxing and pleasurable
Duplo, Lego and other construction kits	18 months +	Fine motor skills	Fun!; achieving an end model, continues their own hobby or like for something, e.g. dinosaur, plane, car, gadget, etc.	Used to show manual dexterity and ability to follow instructions
Painting and colouring	6 months +	Fine motor skills; problem solving; imagination	Fun!; relaxing; allows for non-verbal expression of feelings, frustration, etc.; encourages trying and testing of different styles and skills	Can be used for any child disabled or non-disabled; can be used with any age: finger painting, brush work or specific kits (paint by numbers)

continued

Table 4.1 cont.

Type of normalizing play activity offered	Age suitability	Supports area of development	Experienced as important by the child in the following ways	Recognized as valuable in other ways specific to children in hospital
Hospital play	18 months +	Cognitive; social; understanding of roles, experiences, etc.	Can allow children to explore situations they may encounter at a later point in life – these 'practised' experiences may be valuable to the child in the event of him or her receiving hospital treatment in the future	Allows children to express and explore complex or difficult emotions, experiences or information; adults may be given an insight into a child's experiences of hospital staff and treatment, etc.; to work through phobias, anxieties, etc.
Small world play	12–18 months +	Cognitive; social; fine motor skills	Fun!; allows imagination to flow freely; if familiar toys, characters or scenarios are created this type of play can be very comforting for small children	Allows child to have a sense of control over small world characters and created scenarios; children are often observed to 'work through' difficult issues or situations through the characters created within small world play

Table 4.1 cont.

Type of normalizing play activity offered	Age suitability	Supports area of development	Experienced as important by the child in the following ways	Recognized as valuable in other ways specific to children in hospital
Jigsaw puzzles	12 months +	Fine motor skills	Working towards an achievable end goal, sometimes unseen until you have completed it; also can lend itself to social development if done as a pair or in a group	Allows for the completion of a task; is task specific and is not open-ended; tests patience, tolerance and manual dexterity/observation
Board games	4 years +	Social – encourages awareness of rules, turn-taking, etc.	Fosters good social skills; gives children experiences of winning and losing, turn-taking, problem solving, etc.	Can provide familiarity, renewed control or order to a situation within which sick children may feel very out of control; a good medium around and over which relationships, conversations and friendships can be formed and encouraged
Large physical play/games	Any age	Motor – fine and gross	Provides an outlet for excess energy; encourages children to learn the extremes and limits of what their body can do; gives children a sense of freedom	Encourages children to 'let off steam' and is therefore relaxing and a good release of pent-up anxiety or frustration; supports physical development and can be key in regaining skills lost or impaired by the child's illness

Play rooms: a haven for sick children

Within the set-up of an average hospital ward, most play specialists will be involved, at least for some of their time, in planning, overseeing or actively running play activities on offer in a ward playroom. Depending on the size of their working area, they may be responsible for providing sessions open to large numbers of children. These open access sessions are extremely important for children staying in hospital for any length of time – short or long – because they offer a powerful communication to children that not only is play allowed here, but it is positively encouraged and accepted as being an important part of a child's daily life and routine. The cues sent out by the provision of normalizing play suggest to children that they have permission to play and recognize that this is both a vital need – especially in the face of situations that may bring about additional stress – and a basic right, as defined within the UN Convention of the Rights of the Child 1990. By providing play spaces and normalizing activities for children when they are in hospital the play specialist can aim to provide them with a means to cope with stress and the differences between the normality of home and the strangeness of their new environment, as we have previously discussed.

Hospital is an environment commonly perceived as being traumatic and distressing for children and young people. A less common perception – or one that is considered to be of less significance perhaps – may be the risks to children of the boredom that can set in during a stay in hospital, or a lengthy wait to see the doctor. Boredom can be a significant stressor in itself for some children in hospital or even being seen at their local healthcare centre. Therefore in addition to providing the bridge between comfort and strangeness, an important function of normalizing play for some children will include the reduction of boredom (Lansdown 1996). While it is widely recognized that children need to experience a degree of boredom in life so as to learn how to become self-motivated in their play and learning, there is a danger that during a period of illness, if they are not helped to manage their feelings they will get stuck in a rut. The hospital ward can seem to be the hub of activity, yet as passive observers of this busyness, when unwell and less physically active (Harvey and Hales-Tooke 1972; Jolly 1981; Lansdown 1996), children can easily struggle or become overwhelmed by the experience of boredom and this can lead to an increase in stress, anxiety or despondency that could give way to depression.

Without adequate access to stimulating activities, children can begin to worry or become anxious about the issues they may face by being ill, whether they are receiving treatment in hospital or at home. Similarly, boredom may cause them to become destructive or frustrated in their behaviour towards possessions, other people or themselves. Therefore by having open – or at least regular – access to the ward playroom, or by the provision of one-to-one play sessions with the play specialist, the potential for children to become bored can be effectively prevented and as a result their experience of stress and anxiety can be significantly reduced.

Another important function of ward playrooms and of normal, familiar play activities for sick children is that it can give them a renewed sense of control at a time and in an environment that strips many children of control over their bodies and the decisions affecting them. In the playroom, children can make positive choices about what they do with their time and can create a space through their own decisions around play activities within which they feel safe, able to cope and able to command a degree of mastery, and where they can begin to take on or process complex, worrying or unpleasant thoughts or information.

Most playrooms in hospitals provide a home corner and also the opportunity for some sort of hospital play – whether this is small world play with little figures and a model hospital or a 'hospital corner' for pretend play. These play spaces actively allow and encourage children to safely explore their hospital experiences through play and can allow play staff to observe how well they are managing the impact of their hospital admission and treatment. Playrooms are often a place where messy play and large-scale creative play is encouraged, recognizing that children sometimes need to express their feelings and frustrations through the manipulation of art material such as paint, playdough or clay or that achieving a goal by creating an object, model or painting, and by doing so boosting a child's self-esteem, is of great importance.

Most positively, playrooms in hospitals and waiting areas in healthcare centres and clinics provide a place for the continuation of social development. Hospital admission, while having the potential to provide the child with many harmful experiences, may also present children with many opportunities for befriending other children and engaging with them on a positive and pleasurable level (Harvey and Hales-Tooke 1972; Weller 1980; Lansdown 1996). Playrooms powerfully communicate to children that they are not alone, can share their stay in hospital with peers in a similar position and can have fun playing and socializing in spite of any concerns there may be around their health, treatment and wellbeing.

One-to-one working

While the open access ward playroom is often a focus of a majority of the normalizing play on offer by play specialists, as previously mentioned, they also have responsibility for providing individual sessions and resources for the children on their wards who are restricted to their bed or who have specific or significant needs. These children are likely to have been identified as being a priority for the involvement of the play specialist. For those play specialists who are not based in the hospital setting, but who take referrals for working with a range of children in the community, for example, planning and providing normalizing play in one-to-one play sessions may well constitute a significant part of their day-to-day work.

Patients who are most often seen as a priority to the play specialist generally tend to be children who are in isolation due to an infection or immune deficiency, children who are in hospital on a long-term basis, children who are struggling with a particular aspect of their hospital experience, children who are already recognized as being developmentally delayed for some reason, children who do not have a parent or significant carer staying with them or those children who have other known specific needs. Broadly speaking these children can be identified as being more significantly at risk of having their normal development impaired somehow by their treatment, diagnosis or hospital stay. For such children as these it is necessary, first, to establish the greatest area of need – usually a particular area of their development – and planning normalizing play activities that can be provided to support and enhance the continuation or maintenance of good development in that area (Lansdown 1996).

Where the needs of children who are in isolation are being considered or where there is a concern around their social wellbeing, it is not necessarily crucial to plan overtly therapeutic play sessions as the child's greatest need may be just to have more social contact and an opportunity to build up a sense of trust with someone. On the basis that play is a great icebreaker, normalizing play activities can provide a way to encourage a relationship of trust between the child and play specialist. This in turn can encourage and facilitate good communication through which children can begin to understand and cope with their hospital experiences as effectively as possible. Therefore while for some children play activities may be very specifically planned to support an aspect or multiple aspects of their development, it may sometimes be the case that the main aim of the play specialist is to encourage positive social interaction with the child, or maybe even just to have some really good fun!

Hospital play

Depending on the age of the child and his or her particular needs, hospital play may take the form of imaginative games, possibly taking place in a specifically themed 'hospital corner' in the ward or hospital playroom, using hospital-related dressing-up clothes, dolls, soft toys or other children (in the case of a 'hospital corner' that is open access and to which a group of children are naturally and freely drawn together to play), play doctor's kits and possibly some real hospital equipment (syringes, stethoscopes, etc.). Given access to such resources and the freedom to play, children are able to 'become' doctors, nurses or other characters that they may have encountered during their illness and its treatment. They may choose to immerse themselves in this activity in order to play around their experiences of being ill, being made better or being in hospital.

Alternatively hospital play may take the form of so-called 'small world play', whereby the child is given access to a model of a hospital, character figures and possibly emergency vehicles. The child is then allowed to play through his or her real or perceived experiences through the characters before him or her. Such small world play allows children not only to use their imagination, but also encourages a sense of mastery over the scenario they are building up through their play.

The provision of specifically hospital-themed play (and also postprocedural play, see below) straddles both arenas of normalizing play and the provision of emotional support through play. This dual identity is because it is often set up as an open access activity – albeit taking a number of different forms – in a ward playroom or waiting area in which children can play freely without specific guidance from the play specialist. For this reason it is being included in this section of the book.

Hospital play can have a particularly therapeutic value for sick children, thereby contributing to the care of their emotional wellbeing. Its value therefore needs to be remembered when considering how the play specialist is best able to support sick children emotionally. Some hospital play resources may well be used to explore issues related to a child's experiences of being in hospital within a structured play session with the play specialist, which it itself may have a very specific slant, purpose or planned outcome.

Hospital play encourages children to be able to work through difficult or unpleasant scenarios – real or imagined. As a result, children can also begin to change and adapt their understanding of and reactions to their experiences. Even if a child is quite closely observed at play, achieving a sense of resolution to the difficulties he or she may have faced can often happen without much – if any – explicit adult input.

Post-procedural and 'post-traumatic event' play

If children have experienced high levels of stress or trauma, they may well be observed to explore complex issues connected with those experiences or their emotional responses to them through play activities. It is not recommended that play specialists set out with the intention of tackling issues of trauma with children head-on or analysing children's behaviour during play without collaboration, specific advice, direction or supervision from a colleague such as a clinical psychologist.

However, acknowledging, observing and where necessary recording the things with which children appear to be grappling or that they are exploring through their play activities is important, as is sharing these observations appropriately with others within the multidisciplinary team. Such observations, as well as any carefully considered interventions on the part of the play specialist, may be key to understanding the issues children may be facing. They may also powerfully demonstrate their ability to cope – or otherwise – with potentially stressful experiences in the future or how well they may take on and manage complex information and emotions.

By allowing children free access to a full range of play activities within the playroom, or to have regular play sessions at their bedside, the play specialist gives them the opportunity to face or explore difficult issues at their own pace, through whatever medium with which they are comfortable. Feelings of anger or frustration may not be explicitly discussed, but a child may vigorously knead or bash a pile of playdough, for example, or build towers or sandcastles that are then enthusiastically destroyed, or draw pictures that are scribbled out or torn up.

When planning and undertaking play provision for children who have faced traumatic, distressing or unpleasant experiences, the play specialist will need to employ great sensitivity to their needs. By carefully observing issues, emotions or memories that children may well explore while they are playing, he or she will respond to their needs using a variety of guided hospital or unstructured normalizing play activities. All this will need to be done while still carefully observing any professional boundaries existing within the multidisciplinary team.

Normalizing play to observe or assess children's behaviour

> An open and receptive state of mind and an ability to record (mentally and on paper) the fine detail of a child's behaviour both involve skills and attitudes which have to be acquired. (Fawcett 1996, pp.106–7)

The training of play specialists requires a firm foundation knowledge and understanding of children's development. It also contains a number of assignments with a learning outcome, at least in part, of acquiring and honing observational and recording skills, of the kind to which Fawcett makes reference in the above statement. Normalizing play sessions, both one-to-one and group activities, can often provide natural and suitable opportunities for observing children's behaviour and reactions to being in hospital, and understanding their level of development or ability. The two key elements of the play specialist's prior knowledge and training, when brought together should enable play specialists to be able competently – and sometimes quite instinctively – to observe and assess the level of development and the behaviour of the children and young people with whom they work.

Play specialists are often able to recognize normal as well as impaired or disrupted development, behaviour and adverse reactions to illness and hospitalization. The level of skill and expertise required for this should be duly acknowledged although all too often it goes unnoticed by those who might already be inclined to dismiss or fail to see the central significance of play for sick children. Play specialists are often observed themselves to have an almost intuitive ability to approach and 'read' the behaviour and wellbeing of a child and then to be able to gauge how well that child will cope with medical information that is to be shared or a procedure that is to be carried out, for example.

These days, however, it is often necessary – or at least desirable – to be able to provide evidence in support of any observations that might be made and a purely instinctive understanding of children is all too often in danger of having its validity overlooked or reduced by colleagues and other professionals. An entirely instinctive approach to working with sick children could count against play specialists in a world and professional environment that very often demands measurable or quantifiable evidence upon which to base practice and indeed, with a wider view, increased funding or support.

While it is not within the play specialist's role to observe children and analyse anything symbolic in their playful behaviour (this would be more likely to come under the remit of a play therapist or psychologist), it is perfectly acceptable and often very necessary to record any observations that are thought to be significant, adding a note of whether these match the expectations that may be held for a child at a certain age or of a particularly ability. Behavioural concerns could also be noted in this manner.

Harvey (in Azarnoff 1986) discusses the value of observing children engaged in painting and art-based activities for a number of reasons. While the issue of interpreting and 'reading' children's drawings and paintings is discussed, what is more pertinent here is using art sessions as a means to observe children, who become immersed in a relaxed state brought about by the opportunity to paint or draw and begin to express how they are feeling or what they are experiencing at that time. Harvey highlights the working method of the play specialist as always striking a very fine balance between 'skilled intervention and non-intervention' and suggests that children's artwork provides a window into their minds in three main ways, namely: the overt (not interpreted) content of the pictures themselves; the things that children say to themselves whilst they paint or draw – their own narrative of their experiences; or what they say to the adults around them about the content of their artwork. Both Lansdown (1996) and Bluebond-Langner (1978) have also discussed in some detail both the significance of looking at children's drawings and also looking at children whilst they are drawing so as to gain an insight into their frame of mind or outlook on a given situation.

It is also the case that we live and work in an age of litigation, blame and high-profile child protection cases, all of which mean that it is becoming more common for healthcare professionals to be called to account for their work or provide evidence in legal proceedings concerned with children with whom they may have worked. In this specific scenario, written evidence, observational accounts of behaviour or details that have been recorded will come under significant scrutiny. Therefore maintaining some skills in recording and presenting observations of children's behaviour or assessments of their abilities is important for all those engaged in working with children regardless of the specific setting. In some cases it may be advantageous to employ a recognized observational technique and to write up any observations in an accepted form. If this is not readily available or appropriate, it is recommended that supervision should be sought from colleagues or a manager, since largely, record keeping must be formulaic and rock solid in both content and presentation.

Fawcett (1996) discusses a number of established methods of child observation in detail. In doing so she highlights the fact that the method selected will depend very much upon the setting in which a professional is observing children, and the outcome that is sought from making an observation. Gaining familiarity and competence in using various observation methods both to assess children's abilities, coping or behavioural difficulties and in order to best plan play activities to support the continuation of their normal development is key for play specialists.

'Dovetailing'

According to Lansdown (1996, p.69), 'one of the key characteristics of play specialists is their role as members of a team'. Sometimes normalizing play can be provided that enhances or aids the continuation of work already begun by other healthcare professionals. In this case normalizing play sessions would be closely planned with other members of the child's multidisciplinary team. The play specialist may provide painting at the child's bedside, for example, but will have communicated with the child's physiotherapist or occupational therapist over the most desirable way for the child to hold a paintbrush or may arrange the room so that the child is encouraged to stand at an easel – a continuation of his or her physiotherapy session – rather than sitting for prolonged periods in bed.

The most important feature of this type of planned one-to-one work is that it is regularly provided and continuity is maintained. On a busy hospital ward where children may be seen by many professionals over the course of each day, not to mention the variables brought about by the child's illness and treatment, maintaining this

At the age of two years and four months, Edward became acutely unwell and was diagnosed with meningococcal meningitis. He was critically unwell for several weeks, being cared for in a paediatric intensive care unit and undergoing a procedure on his legs and arms called a fasciotomy. In Edward's case this involved deep cuts being made to the muscles of the lower legs and forearms, a procedure that was carried out in order to relieve the enormous pressure created by significant swelling and a build up of fluid – the body's response to the catastrophic infection in his body – which threatened to cut off the blood supply to his legs and arms, fingers and toes.

After his meningitis had been successfully treated, Edward was left with wounds from four fasciotomy sites, including two on his lower legs that had left him with some nerve damage which, in turn, had an effect on his balance and ability to walk or stand. Edward was seen on a daily basis by the physiotherapist who helped him regain the ability to use his legs. Because these sessions were painful and stressful for Edward, the physiotherapist requested the input of the play specialist in her daily contact with him. Together the play specialist and physiotherapist devised physical games that included the necessary stretches and exercises to aid Edward's physical recovery. They also included elements of distraction into the session so that, for example, instead of simply insisting that Edward stand for a period of time – which he found uncomfortable – he was encouraged to stand and throw a ball at a target game. With the new elements of distraction and an enjoyable play activity, Edward's physiotherapy sessions were more bearable for him, meaning he was more inclined to be compliant and cooperative.

In addition to the cooperative working with the physiotherapist, the play specialist was able to incorpate elements of the sessions into Edward's play activities in the ward playroom at other times. For example he was encouraged to paint at an easel – an activity he greatly enjoyed – but instead of sitting to do this he was helped to stand in the position demonstrated to play staff by the physiotherapist. This helped to strengthen the weakened muscles in his legs, and also increased his confidence in supporting his own weight once again.

continuity can be the biggest challenge to the provision of good quality, regularly provided normalizing play. In areas where play is not regarded as a priority service in its own right this may be an even more significant issue and requires the profile of play in hospital to be raised quite considerably.

Play specialists regularly working with children with the aim of supporting and encouraging them in their development should be expected to contribute a description of their input in a child's notes and would be advised to be prepared to show some sort of plan for their work with individual children. There is currently no widely accepted type of planning document in use by play specialists and therefore play teams are more often than not required to create their own paperwork. This should include a space for some description of the individual child's specific needs, the aim or desirable outcome as a result of the play specialist's involvement, and the activities that may be provided with this aim in mind.

If play specialists are able to attend any ward or team planning meetings either for individual children or the whole ward it would be advantageous both to the play specialist and the wider team. Such opportunities allow for the exchange of information and ideas on how best to respond to the individual needs of the children being cared for. They also provide a forum for discussion around approaches to the needs and difficulties faced by children, families and staff alike.

A firm foundation

In conclusion then, while the role of the play specialist is understood to be diverse and multifaceted, it is the provision of normalizing play that lays down the grass roots for the provision of any further specialized play provided for sick children and young people. Without this, the value of any other play-based provision offered is greatly diminished since normalizing play activities provide such a robust means to the creation of trust, insight and a relationship with the child. The delivery of play in one-to-one planned sessions as well as

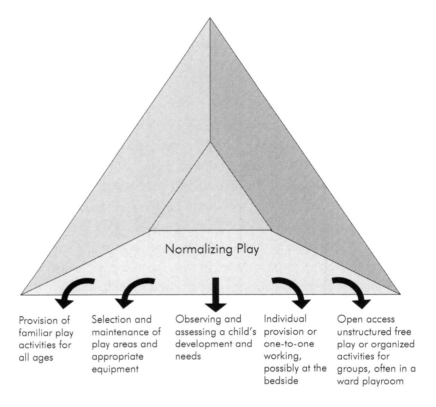

Figure 4.1 The provision of normalizing play

within a well-run playroom or waiting area gives important cues to the child that play is valued and encouraged. It communicates to children that healthcare settings can be places of safety and recovery, where their needs will be recognized and met.

The provision of normalizing play must be considered to be crucial when it is accepted that it underpins all other areas of work undertaken by play specialists. It could even be argued that their practice is at risk of being impaired somehow if this provision is not a valued part of that work. By the provision of comforting and familiar play activities, there is more of a possibility for greater, more specialized therapeutic intervention through play.

Normalizing play is therefore the crucial, solid foundation upon which the broader and more varied role of the play specialist is built. The more specialized aspects of play for sick children and the breadth of the work undertaken by play specialists is constantly changing and evolving. In spite of this it is essential that the importance of normalizing play must not be forgotten or overlooked, if only for the sake of children receiving quality care and support.

The more specialized areas of play work with sick children may sometimes seem to be more exciting, more stimulating or more motivating by the immediate results observed. Without the backdrop of normalizing play, however, these results would be less forthcoming since it is the access to familiar and comforting play that allows children to be more receptive to the emotional support offered or information shared with the aim of helping them cope as well as possible with invasive procedures, traumatic diagnoses or stressful experiences.

5

Emotional Support and the 'Art' of Distraction

The guiding principle which emerges for the care of children in hospital is that while the child must, of course, undergo the necessary investigations and treatment for the condition from which he is suffering, he should be subjected to the least possible disturbance. (Platt 1959, p.4)

Body or soul...or both?

The ancient Greek philosopher, Plato, observed that a great error made by physicians of the day was the tendency to 'separate the mind from the body'. Indeed, it is very often still the case that the needs of people who are unwell and in hospital are defined largely or even exclusively by their physical condition and its treatment, while their emotional, social and psychological needs are often somewhat overlooked or at least viewed as being quite separate to their physical needs.

This approach to people who are ill – known as the 'medical model' – concerns itself largely with the diagnosis and definition of disease, relying mainly upon physical signs and symptoms of illness and the treatment of a condition with drugs in order to bring about a change in the patient's state of health. It is a scientific, evidence-based approach to the care of people who are sick. Within the context of the medical model, all issues relating to health and illness are viewed and understood to be determined only by the physical processes within the body. The mind is seen as an extended function of the nervous system and not independently influential over our sense of health or wellbeing (Marks *et al.* 2000). Despite greater encouragement given to healthcare professionals to consider the other less physiological influences on health and wellbeing, the medical model tends generally to define how patients are treated within most health service provision today.

The medical model significantly shapes the training and therefore the approach of many medical professionals, particularly doctors and, while this approach can be very valuable in terms of efficient diagnosis and effective treatment, it can lead to attention being almost exclusively focused on patients' physical condition, while little or no consideration is given to any other significant aspects of their lives. There is consequently a danger that medical professionals may neglect to consider the psychological, social or emotional needs of the patient, or the important aspects of an individual's lifestyle that may affect his or her health or ability to recover from an illness. In the worst-case scenario, this approach can lead to individuals feeling that they are not judged, valued or understood on any basis other than their physical needs or ailments. A powerful example of this is given by Jolly (1981) who recounts a conversation with a little boy in hospital who himself sagely observed: 'They looked at my ears, they looked at my throat, they looked at my tummy, but they didn't look at me' (p.9).

In contrast, the social model of health focuses on the person in a holistic way, not merely defining that person by an ailment, or an impairment or seeing him or her as something to be 'fixed' or alternatively to be 'pitied' by others. By means of an understanding of child development and the benefits of play to all areas of that development, the play specialist's approach values individuals rather than categorizing them or limiting them according to their condition and its effects. The play specialist therefore has a role in the multidisciplinary team to bring balance to the medicalized approach that can be a dominant feature of a child's care in a variety of healthcare settings.

Play in its essence is positive. It provides a naturally inclusive and largely undefined environment where children of all ages and abilities can join in. Without disregarding the medical expertise of their colleagues, and while having to work mostly within the restrictions created by a child's physical condition at any given time, the play specialist works to ensure that the needs of the whole child are understood and adequately met. By the general provision of play, the sharing of appropriate information and an overarching aim to safeguard the emotional wellbeing of the child, the play specialist should be a voice within the multidisciplinary team that passionately yet professionally promotes the child's needs as more than just a collection of physical signs, symptoms and solutions.

Cognitive development

For those caring for sick children and young people, being able to offer an appropriate level of support depends very much upon understanding where a child is 'at' in terms of his or her understanding of bodies, health, illness, treatment and recovery. Through his or her training and experience of working with children, the play specialist will have gained solid theoretical knowledge and anecdotal experience of children's cognitive development. Being in possession of such knowledge and having the confidence to use it is a crucial aspect to giving solid, reliable, appropriate and honest information to children, being able to discuss specific issues relating to their health or treatment and gauging how best to support their emotional wellbeing. While greater attention will be paid to the whole area of giving information to children in the chapter that follows, it is important to note here that the dual aspects of the role of the play specialist of emotional support and imparting information dovetail very closely with each other.

With this in mind then, it is important to accept that to give a child adequate information about his or her body, condition and treatment in an appropriate manner is in itself a form of emotional support. If children feel that the adults around them are communicating with them, they will experience less distress or anxiety than if they sense that details of their illness or situation are somehow being concealed from them. When supporting a child through a difficult medical procedure, for example, the play specialist's aim should therefore always be in the first instance to give adequate, accurate and clear information to the child, and then to follow this up with appropriate and effective emotional support, including distraction during the procedure. While both the giving of information and emotional support can be – and often are – seen or delivered as separate aspects of the play services offered to sick children, for a variety of reasons, the optimal and therefore most desirable approach by the play specialist is to include both aspects within the more specialized interactions that they have with their patients.

Are you talking to me...?

It is often assumed – and sometimes observed – that sick children quickly develop an accelerated understanding of their bodies, state of health and treatment (Eiser 1995; Lansdown 1996), especially those whose condition is chronic or persistent. The same may also be said for children who become acutely ill since, whether they are acutely or chronically sick, children are remarkably capable of very quickly picking up on the conversations that happen around them while their condition is being discussed, assessed or treated.

That said, however, it is dangerous to make the assumption that children will somehow instinctively know and understand all that is happening to them if or when they become unwell. This knowledge and understanding depends on a great many factors including age, experience, formal learning, communication styles within families and the individual child's general interest or awareness of his or her own body, for example.

In addition to a general understanding of how children's cognitive ability develops, it is key that play specialists are familiar with the recognized areas or stages of understanding encountered by children specifically in relation to health and illness. This knowledge allows for any information sharing and emotional support to be pitched at an appropriate level and will enable the play specialist to be able to adapt his or her style of work to meet the needs of the children with whom he or she works on an individual basis.

While considering what and how children learn about illness, health and how their bodies work, it is important to consider the potential for there to be emotional difficulties encountered by children if they feel that they have not been given adequate, appropriate or reliable information relating to their health or the treatment that they are going to receive.

There are two common dangers encountered in this context. The first is that too little information will be offered to the child or young person who is ill. By underestimating their level of cognitive development or out of a desire to protect them from further distress, parents and sometimes medical staff may run a significant risk of giving children – especially those who are quite young – too basic an explanation of why they are ill ('it's your heart that is poorly'), thinking that this is all that the child requires. Such a motivation to not unduly worry or upset children is understandable, but it could be the case that, in fact, to give inadequate information to children may cause them greater anxiety as it risks introducing new and sometimes quite abstract concepts ('what/where *IS* my heart?!') as well as a worrying but vague sense that all is not well.

Second, there is the need to consider the opposite issue to this. Here, too much information is given and either the child is overwhelmed by all that he or she has been told or is simply unable to process the wave of facts, figures, new words or plans in which he or she has been immersed. This is often seen in the case of those 'knowledgeable' children who have a chronic or persistent illness, especially if it is a condition that is largely managed by the family in the home setting as well as within the hospital (diabetes or cystic fibrosis would present as two reasonable examples). These children can often rattle off a list of drugs or treatments as long their arm, and may even be able to tell you fairly reliably what they do, how many times a day they must be taken and various other seemingly competent facts.

Cracks start to appear in the veneer of apparent competence, however, when, for example, children are asked about why they must take certain medication or to give details about what their condition actually is. At these points, it is not uncommon to find that children with chronic diseases are at a loss to provide such an explanation. While it is assumed that they know and understand a lot – or at least enough – about their condition, it is often the case that chronically ill children are actually rather ill-informed about all aspects of their condition and its treatment (Eiser 1990). This may offer an explanation as to why this group of children, having undergone a significant amount of medical procedures, sometimes struggle with phobias or fears in specific contexts, or demonstrate challenging behaviour in the face of treatment. Sometimes this is found to be at least in part because they do not adequately understand the reasons why a certain procedure must go ahead. Once children's ability to understand and make sense of their condition is redressed they can often be helped to be more compliant with various aspects of their treatment.

The play specialist involved in talking about such issues with children will usually start by establishing the child's level of understanding. This is often done by simply asking the children to explain what they already know about why they are in hospital, particularly in the case of a child who is acutely ill or has been newly diagnosed with a condition. By discovering a child's existing level of knowledge, the play specialist can begin to tailor further information sharing on a very individual basis. For example, in continuing with our example of the child with a 'poorly heart', it is quite likely that the play specialist will begin with some basic information around the function of the heart, how it works and where it is located. With this baseline information in place, the child can be helped to understand better – at an appropriate level – not only what the heart is for and how it works, but what it means to have a heart that is actually not working as it should, as well as how the adults caring for him or her are going to aim to alleviate the problems caused by having a 'heart that is poorly'.

By the means of a sensitive, well-informed and insightful approach, the play specialist does not only aim to give an appropriate amount of information to the child. By means of that information giving, he or she also effectively offers the child a good level of emotional support, by aiming to reduce the risk of the child experiencing undue stress or anxiety.

The play specialist was asked to work with Maya, an eight-year-old girl with cystic fibrosis (CF), because she was showing signs of being anxious during outpatient appointments and had also been attention-seeking during a recent admission to the medical ward. She gave the impression of being confident and knowledgeable and could reel off a lot of impressive-sounding information about her medicines and their various functions. However, after further discussion with Maya, it became clear that her anxiety seemed to be rooted in the sense that she did not really understand certain aspects of her condition. When the play specialist asked her to explain all that she knew about CF, she was at a loss to give any meaningful explanation.

She began to talk about how difficult she found it to explain to other people about her CF, when she didn't really understand the condition herself. She also talked about how it was hard to understand how no one else in her family had CF, even though it had 'come from Mummy' – suggesting to me that she had received and retained a rudimentary explanation of CF as being genetic in its nature. By assessing and establishing how much understanding Maya had of her CF, the play specialist was able to work with her on a project in which information about CF was gathered and presented in a book. This included information about its genetic causes and how CF manifests itself in affected families, as well as the symptoms of and various treatments for CF.

The assumption that Maya was in possession of all the facts about her condition because she was seemingly knowledgeable meant that no one had thought to give her adequate information. This sense of not knowing about something so central to her everyday life had eventually become stressful and almost unbearable for Maya.

Supporting sick children

In considering how to offer the best possible level of appropriate and effective emotional support to sick children and young people, it is important to identify some of the reasons why those children might specifically require that support. A study by Moos and Tsu (1977), discussed by Lansdown (1996), proposes that there are six factors that should be considered when working with physically ill patients. These should be taken into account when acknowledging the possibility that children and their families in hospital and other healthcare settings may well encounter stressful, unpleasant or downright traumatic experiences. Although not all of the following will necessarily be pertinent to all patients, they are still worth bearing in mind when aiming to offer emotional support in a variety of ways.

Difficult or stressful tasks facing children and their families may include:

• dealing with pain or being incapacitated

• dealing with the hospital environment and developing relationships with the hospital staff

• managing feelings of anxiety, resentment and isolation; preserving emotional balance

• preserving relationships with family and friends

• preparing for an uncertain future.

With these factors put forward by Moos and Tsu in mind, what follows are some of the possible reasons why the experience of being unwell and in hospital may be stressful, difficult or unpleasant for children, young people and their families.

Environmental or contextual stress within hospital/healthcare settings

In the introduction to Susan Harvey and Ann Hales-Tooke's book *Play in Hospital* (1972), Dr David Morris outlines the fact that children face a very stressful scenario when they enter the world of the hospital. Morris acknowledges the adjustments children face having to make in the light of the 'bewildering array of different sounds, smells and sights' (p.15) that this strange environment brings with it. Indeed, Ann Hales-Tooke, discussing children's self-reported reactions to their stay in hospital, comments on the striking number who mentioned the unpleasant smell of the hospital including one who described that experience saying: 'The first thing I noticed was the smell and my tummy felt quite upside down' (Hales-Tooke 1973, p.79).

Further to this however, hospital must be recognized as being a place where 'strange, often frightening and painful things are done' to children (Harvey and Hales-Tooke 1972, p.15) and therefore a sick child's need for appropriate and adequate emotional support is acknowledged. While Morris's words specifically address the hospital environment, his thoughts and observations can be taken as relevant also to other healthcare settings. While Morris was writing some 35 years ago or more, and in spite of the fact that the National Health Service generally – along with many more specific aspects of children's healthcare – has changed phenomenally in this time, his observations, none the less, remain relevant for children visiting or staying in a hospital today. The challenge for children of coping with the hospital experience that Morris describes may very well be the same today as it was for children a generation or two ago.

Specific children's hospitals and designated children's wards have put in a great amount of effort to make their waiting, treatment and residential areas 'child-friendly' by minimizing as far as possible anything that presents itself to be overly clinical. Purpose-built children's units and hospices, artwork on the walls, open-plan ward areas, and changes to staff uniform – including, even, the almost-total ban on doctors wearing white coats – are all examples of the recognition that children may significantly benefit from a very different healthcare environment to their adult counterparts. However, it is still necessary to acknowledge that while these features may all improve the experience of a child in whatever the given setting, it is still an environment that is very different to the familiar and comfortable surroundings of home, and therefore what the child may experience whilst being cared for in that setting may still be unpleasant or distressing for a wide variety of reasons. The environment can certainly enhance a child's sense of wellbeing, but his or her experience of illness and being made well still brings with it a great many other potential stressors.

Seeing other children or adults who are ill

Great care is often taken to protect children particularly from seeing things that may be distressing or frightening, both to observe or to imagine. Medical procedures, for example, tend to happen away from an open ward area and are often carried out in a treatment room. This is as much for the benefit of other children in the ward as it is for preserving the dignity of the child who requires the medical intervention. It is, however, impossible to totally shield children from the reality of the experiences of their peers during their stay in hospital. Therefore there is a certain inevitability that children will overhear, see or indeed imagine things that they find disturbing, or at the very least, interesting while they are surrounded by others going through their own treatment.

Hales-Tooke (1973) asked children to describe the things that were significant to them about being in hospital. The children she spoke to told her of their distress at seeing 'little babies being injected' or other children crying and one child graphically recounted feelings of fear at seeing distressing sights on arriving at hospital, saying:

> When we went through the front door [of the hospital] I was not scared or worried, but when we went down the second corridor, through an open door I saw an unconscious woman lying on a trolley. I thought she was dead and I was very scared. (Hales-Tooke 1973, p.80)

These experiences – in particular the above example of children witnessing not just the other children in their children's ward area, but also their awareness of adult patients and the distress that this caused – all serve as a reminder that consideration is due for the reality that children often observe and take in more than may be realized. This issue may be worth careful consideration for those working with children who receive treatment or consultation in a general Accident and Emergency department, general Outpatients or whilst accompanying children to an operating theatre, the workload of which includes both adults and children. Children may need a significant amount of reassurance or extra preparation for the things they may see or hear, or – particularly in the case of A&E – some post-procedural-type discussion to help them understand the things that may have worried or frightened them.

Cook (1999) also uses the specific example of children receiving treatment in the intensive care unit when considering the upsetting things that children are at risk of witnessing. While research suggests that children have little or no memory of their own acute phase of their treatment in the ICU, it is during their time of recovery and withdrawal from sedating drugs that staff should be most aware of what they are likely to witness. Cook urges that as soon as they are well enough, children should be moved to a different area in order to 'protect them from sights and sounds that may be frightening' (p.166).

An important part of the play specialist's role in offering emotional support includes assisting children in adjusting to the strangeness of the hospital environment and in expressing and coping with the things that may be frightening, unpleasant or distressing to witness. While confidentiality prevents discussion about other patients in any detail, it is often necessary to offer some reassurance or explanation to a child about what may be happening to another child on the ward, or to another patient elsewhere in the hospital. It may simply be to recognize what the child has seen or overheard, and to acknowledge that being aware of another child crying or vomiting, for example, is not pleasant for anyone and to offer the child appropriate reassurance. Once such a discussion has taken place, distraction in the form of an alternative activity or change of environment may be the most helpful approach.

Acknowledging children's reaction to others who are ill or being treated in hospital need not always be seen as a wholly difficult or negative thing. Children are naturally inquisitive and it is positive to encourage this innate sense of interest in their immediate and the wider environment. In some cases, by exploring or observing this new environment, children encounter a whole new world of information and experiences when they come into hospital and particularly when they talk to one another. The conversations between children sometimes taking place in the play area, can be highly insightful and highlight how children can quite naturally inform and support each other during their period of illness and treatment.

Another part of the play specialist's role could be taking this natural befriending to a slightly higher level by facilitating a more organized programme of peer support. This may naturally grow from friendships simply formed while children are inpatients together. Alternatively, in some settings this could be set up more deliberately, such as in the case of an older or more experienced patient being introduced to a newly diagnosed or younger patient. This could be especially valuable if both patients have the same condition, such as diabetes or asthma, or have undergone the same course of medical or surgical treatment. (N.B. A programme of peer support, such as in the case of this sort of example, would need to be carefully set up so that patient confidentiality can be correctly observed.)

Volume of staff

When children are exposed to a strange new environment such as that presented by the hospital or walk-in healthcare centre, or even on a first visit to a hospice, respite or rehabilitation centre, for example, one factor that could cause them significant stress is the sheer number of new people they will see or meet there (Lansdown 1996;

Hubbuck 2003). Lansdown (referring to a study by Cleary 1992) suggests that a child may be looked after by up to eight nurses across the span of a day and a night, 'with the weekly total being no fewer than 116 nurses', (p.41) not to mention all the medical and ancillary staff on top of this number. For those familiar with the working environment of the hospital and its personnel, the impact of this issue as a possible stressor could be underestimated, yet it should be recognized that children could well feel quite overwhelmed by the sheer number of people they will encounter, because – at least to begin with – 'everyone is a stranger to the child' (Hales-Tooke 1973, p.78).

Adults are quite accustomed to meeting and interacting on a daily basis with a great many people whom they do not necessarily know. Since social interaction is something that is learned and developed over a significant period of time most people manage to negotiate their way through these interactions fairly easily. However, for a lot of children, particularly younger children, being exposed to many new faces and having to interact with unfamiliar people can be quite overwhelming, and for some will be quite a frightening and upsetting experience. Their distress could be more keenly felt if it is coupled with the already stressful experience of being ill or having suffered an injury of some kind. A child's distress inevitably will increase if he or she is suddenly expected to tolerate more than just a simple set of straightforward verbal interactions from all the strangers around him or her.

Imagine if you will, that these new people not only want to talk, but also may want examine the child, touch him or her in a way that is neither comfortable nor familiar, and possibly to take blood or administer treatment by inserting a needle under his or her skin. For the child who may really only be used to interacting and being physically cared for by an intimate circle of family members and close friends, this experience could be bewildering and frightening in the extreme.

It is also worth considering the point that children may very well be used to relying on their parents for support and protection from stressful circumstances and experiences, yet at just this point when children can feel at their most vulnerable, their parent or carer wilfully (or so it may well seem to the child) appears to allow this new and bewildering situation to happen, by letting healthcare professionals do the necessary examining and administering of treatment (Belson 1987). While the acceptance of the role of doctors and nurses and their colleagues seems clear to adults, such familiarity with professional roles will not be obvious to children who may not understand why their parents cannot or do not step in and help, support or protect them as they usually would.

The likely effects of encountering such a high volume of staff should be an important consideration of the multidisciplinary team as a whole when thinking about how children are cared for in their setting. It is rarely possible or, in fact, necessary to reduce or limit the number of healthcare personnel with whom sick children and young people have contact whilst they are in hospital. However, at the very least it is probably worth appreciating how being faced with such a range of new faces, job titles and interactions could be overwhelming, especially if there is little or no specific consideration of the need for an adequate level of emotional support required by children in this situation.

When considering the play specialist's response to children who may struggle to cope with the bewildering world of the hospital, for example, Lansdown (1996) makes the suggestion that their role should be as someone who presents as 'a constant' – a familiar, reliable person for children and families in the ever-changing world of nurses and others who come and go according to their different shift patterns and duties.

Hospital/health jargon and language

While children's cognitive development is always progressing and changing and their capacity for grasping new terms and concepts is always expanding, their ability to understand all that they encounter in life is still limited. This means that, in addition to the potential not only for over- or under-informing them about their health and treatment for illness, there is also always the risk that the language used to talk to them in itself could be confusing or misleading.

For those working in healthcare settings, it can be easy to forget how unfamiliar medical terminology may be to those parents and children to whom such jargon-laden language is so new and strange. It is therefore necessary to consider the language that is used around the young patients and their families, as well as when directly addressing them. It may need to be tweaked or changed in order to minimize any distress or confusion that could be caused by the use of hospital or medical jargon. A study by Gaynard *et al.* (1990) brought to light some of the most common language considerations for talking with children in and about hospital. Here three reasons why terms, words or phrases could be problematic formed a discussion that highlighted first, terms that may commonly be used that are potentially ambiguous (i.e. that could be easily misheard, misinterpreted or about which the child may imagine or fantasize), second, terms that are potentially unfamiliar (i.e. that are generally used only within healthcare environments) and third, those that have a 'hard impact' and could therefore quickly evoke feelings of anxiety, panic or distress. Some examples of these can be seen in Table 5.1, along with suggestions of possible changes that could be made to prevent further confusion or distress being caused.

Table 5.1 Language to be considered when talking with children

	A child might hear	A child might think	Improved method of communication
Potentially ambiguous	Dressing/dressing change	Why are they going to undress me? Do I have to change my clothes? Will I be naked?!	'A dressing is another name for your bandages; we need to change the older bandages, and put on some clean new ones.'
	Put you to sleep	Like my cat was put to sleep? It never came back!	'Medicine, called anaesthesia, helps you sleep during your operation so you won't feel anything. It is a special kind of sleep.'
	Flush your IV	Flush it where? Down the toilet?!	'To put some water down your IV tube/cannula, so that it continues to work and stays clean.'
Potentially unfamiliar	Check your 'Obs'		'To measure your temperature to see how warm your body is and to see how fast and how strongly your heart is working.'
	IV/intravenous		'Medicine that works best when it goes right into a vein, usually through a small plastic tube.'
	NBM/nil by mouth		'Nothing to eat or drink (usually before an operation) – your stomach needs to be empty so that you won't be sick while you are asleep for your operation.'

continued

Table 5.1 cont.

	A child might hear	A child might think	Improved method of communication
Hard impact	This part will hurt		'This part (of the procedure or of your body) may feel sore, scratchy, achey, etc.' (or similarly descriptive word, plus if possible a time-frame for the child).
	The medicine will smell/taste bad		'The medicine may taste/smell different to anything you have tasted before. Let me know how it was for you, after you've taken it, OK?'
	Cut/open you up/ make a hole		'The doctor will make a small opening.' Use concrete comparisons such as 'as big as your little finger', as long as these are honest and reliable.

Being overwhelmed by the experience of being unwell, of hospitalization and of treatment

A child's ability to cope during a period of illness varies depending upon whether he or she is struck by a sudden illness that is treatable and therefore relatively temporary, or is living with a chronic disease that may affect every aspect of his or her daily life. These two scenarios present children, families and healthcare professionals with many different considerations and it is therefore worth looking at the different coping strategies children employ in relation to their state of health according to the acute or chronic nature of their illness.

ACUTELY ILL CHILDREN

Admission to hospital can be a disorientating and bewildering experience for children and their parents (Harvey and Hales-Tooke 1972; Weller 1980; Lansdown 1996; Cook 1999). The family may have little or no preparation for their child's admission to hospital for treatment and it may not be possible, at least to begin with, to predict the length of his or her stay. This sense of uncertainty and of being unsettled can be very stressful for everybody, in addition to the unpleasant experience for the child of feeling unwell. Recognition of this stress is essential for all those involved in the care of children who are acutely ill and that the most immediate and important response is first to reassure children and families that they will quickly receive appropriate and effective care. The first impressions that they gain from contact with hospital staff are vital for building a trusting relationship (Cook 1999). Similarly, being given adequate information about the ward environment and being welcomed into the strange new environment they now find themselves in can be very meaningful to families.

If children become unwell at home, they may well see a doctor at their local general practice, healthcare or 'walk-in' centre who, depending on their condition, may refer them for a further consultation, treatment or tests at a local hospital. When children are injured in traumatic circumstances or become severely ill, they will receive emergency treatment in the Accident and Emergency department. If they are already resident in hospital and their condition suddenly deteriorates, they will similarly require emergency treatment on the ward. At these times it is necessary that the physical wellbeing of the child takes precedent over his or her emotional welfare. In these circumstances, medical staff administer care and treatment to the child, one hopes, communicating what they are doing as clearly and effectively as possible to the child, but often without the time or the opportunity to give the child much formal preparation, if any.

As a result of the rush and alarm at this acute stage of their illness, the child may have to endure uncomfortable, invasive or surprisingly painful procedures or interventions. At times like these, there is often little or no opportunity for the adequate provision of necessary preparation or distraction. They may need to have intravenous access established, to have wounds assessed or treated or to unexpectedly have scans or X-rays. At a time like this children are likely to feel an overwhelming sense of their control having been completely lost or at the very least seriously undermined. They may experience extreme levels of fear or panic in addition to feeling very unwell, all in an environment where they may sense high levels of stress or concern, from their parents and possibly also from the staff looking after them.

It is not only during acute or emergency treatment that children may experience great distress and require adequate and appropriate communication and support. Once that acute phase of a child's journey through hospital is over, there is a danger that the need to 'unpack' or re-visit those stressful and potentially traumatic first experiences remains, but goes unacknowledged. This may happen either because it is simply not accepted as being important for children or alternatively a lack of 'post-procedural' discussion results from the rapid turnover of staff on most hospital wards, which could lead to a basic but misguided assumption that 'someone else' will have taken responsibility for having such a discussion with the patient. This assumption could have disastrous results for the child who has encountered a highly stressful experience while receiving emergency treatment. It may mean that the child's experience is never heard, recognized as being significant or understood as potentially having an effect upon how well he or she will go on to cope with future medical procedures.

An example given by Cook (1999) describes a four-year-old girl injured in a road traffic accident in which her mother died. After she was moved from the intensive care unit to the children's ward, the play specialist there noted how the child was being prevented from playing with toy cars, vehicles and specifically a toy ambulance by her grandmother, despite being continually drawn to this toy. When the grandmother had gone home and the play specialist was alone with her, the little girl 'went to the cupboard and took out the ambulance, told the play specialist that Mummy had gone in the ambulance, slammed the doors shut and pushed [it] away saying that Mummy was gone and was not coming back' (p.164). Similarly while playing with the cars (including a red one – the colour of the car she was a passenger in at the time of the crash) she played dramatic 'crash' games, smashing cars and lorries together. The play specialist observed that the child needed to act out the traumatic experience she had gone through, even though her close relatives in their own grief could hardly bear to allow her to think about her experiences.

Children who have been admitted to hospital when they are acutely ill, especially if they have arrived there as an emergency, present particular challenges because of the stress they may have experienced and any trauma with which they may continue to struggle. Play specialists therefore need to accept that those experiences may be highly important and may significantly inform the work undertaken with those children. It may be important on first meeting a child to bear in mind the possibility that he or she may already have had to cope with a lot of stressful experiences in the course of his or her admission to hospital. Finding out the details of such experiences allows the play specialist to tailor the support offered to individual children so that it can be as effective and meaningful as possible. This may involve simply talking and listening to children, encouraging them to share their experiences so that they can move on from them to be able to cope as well as possible with the remainder of their treatment. It may equally involve planning and creating play sessions that may encourage a child to express strong emotions or play through stressful experiences. If it is felt that they need a greater or more specialized level of support, the play specialist may refer children to another member of the multidisciplinary team, such as the clinical psychologist, who can then help them to work through those stressful experiences and any anxiety caused by them.

CHRONICALLY ILL CHILDREN

The term 'chronic' is understood to mean something that continues for a long time or is constantly returning (*Collins English Dictionary* 1999). Therefore 'chronic illness' can be understood to refer to those conditions that are persistent, life-long and those which may require long-term regular treatment. Such treatment may be well managed, at least for quite a high proportion of the time, within the child's home by the family themselves or with the support of community health-care teams. In addition to a high level of everyday care, chronically ill children may require admission to hospital for further treatment, either as a planned part of their care (in the case of children with cystic fibrosis for example, who may have regular prophylactic intra-venous antibiotic treatment) or because their condition worsens, they become acutely unwell and require emergency treatment (in the case of the child with asthma, for example).

Children who have a chronic illness or condition may spend a lot of time in hospital throughout the course of their childhood and may become very familiar within that environment. However, while a lot of attention is paid to supporting children who are in hospital for the first time, there is a worrying potential that rather less consideration will be given to the needs of chronically sick children when their health deteriorates leading to their readmission to hospital (Eiser 1990). This is in spite of the fact that these children may find being admitted to hospital just as stressful, disorientating or traumatic as their acutely ill peers. Indeed they may be inclined to experience more distress because their level of knowledge is already more developed and they are experienced in terms of their expectations of what being in hospital involves. This in itself may give rise to an increase of anxiety in the face of the anticipation of repeated invasive procedures or the development of phobias.

For children familiar with the hospital environment and its potential stressors, the play specialist is often an important figure who provides consistency and reassurance in the ever-changing and busy ward environment. Eiser (1990, p.22) notes that therapeutic play has the 'greatest potential for helping children come to terms with severe illness or disability' and significantly, that children who received support specifically through play showed less disturbance during treatment and a greater acceptance of the possibility of repeatedly returning to hospital.

Therefore it is of great advantage to children regularly admitted to hospital to be able to develop a relationship of trust and confidence with the play specialists they encounter. It is often the case that play specialists in turn aim to build this level of relationship with their patients so that they can continually respond appropriately and sensitively to their ever-changing needs. Once such a relationship is established the play specialist can tailor his or her work to best meet the needs of children as individuals by understanding specifically how to communicate with and respond to them in any given context. Children's needs will be very different in a regular outpatient appointment, for example, where they may be grateful for spending time just playing or 'catching up' with the play specialist, to their needs if they are admitted to hospital because they are acutely ill, feeling fearful, needing sensitive reassurance and support during potentially painful or tedious treatment regimens.

Depending upon their age and level of cognitive development, it is likely at these times of acute or increased ill health that chronically ill children and young people may show signs of frustration, sadness or anger over their condition (Eiser 1990, 1995; Dempsey 2008) and this may need to be addressed by the play specialist and others involved in the child's care. The effect of the persistency of an illness and the ripple effect of how that illness impacts upon so many aspects of the child's life should not be underestimated. Nor should the significance of issues around whether the child's life is limited or threatened by his or her condition, since addressing these issues and others may feature in the play specialist's work with these children through the years.

This approach to offering generalized emotional support, distraction and support specifically during procedure, as well as giving information to these children will inevitably be different to that which is offered to the child admitted to hospital on a one-off basis. By building up sound knowledge of individual children, their behaviour, their particular strengths, weaknesses and interests and the play input to which they are most responsive, the play specialist can also be an important member of the multidisciplinary team and should ideally be involved in planning care according to the child's specific needs.

Children facing issues of death and dying

In Western society today, death in childhood is an uncommon occurrence. Baum (in Goldman 1998) states that for the majority of families – in the Western world at least – thankfully 'the concept of child mortality has been relegated to history' (p.1). Information released by the Office of National Statistics in 2004 revealed that in the UK in 2002 there were 1,376 deaths of children aged between 1 and 14 years giving a death rate in this age group of 15 deaths per 100,000 children. The main causes of death in the same age group were accidents, injury and poisoning and malignant disease, most commonly leukaemia, which together accounted for 44 per cent of the above statistic. Deaths occurring in infancy are higher – though still relatively low and consistently falling (National Statistics 2004) – and largely occur in connection to premature birth and congenital abnormalities. Two thirds of these deaths occur within the first 28 days of life.

Statistics aside, it is also the case that in Westernized society, generally speaking, the subject of death in childhood is something of a taboo subject with which we are generally uncomfortable (Baum, in Goldman 1998), partly because it presents a challenge to commonly held beliefs around children and childhood, and partly because it is something that is greatly feared by parents and carers of children and therefore prevented as far as is at all possible.

Part of this challenge arises from the expectation of the curative powers of modern medicine, and the preventative nature of improved lifestyles, at least in terms of general cleanliness, childhood immunization and recognition of children's health needs. The fact that death in childhood is altogether a rare occurrence also adds to the difficulties that professionals may experience in managing one's reaction in the face of terminal illness or the death of a child when it does occur. As levels of child mortality progressively fall generation after generation to almost unimaginably low levels (Baum, in Goldman 1998) so there is a risk that the numbers of professionals and individuals who can most effectively offer support to families going through the experience of losing a child reduces to a similar degree. These are all issues that present interesting challenges to professionals involved in caring for sick children, especially those who have a life-limiting or life-threatening condition, in a variety of healthcare settings.

The rarity for play specialists of working with a child as they are dying

Just as it is important to accept that death in childhood happens rarely, even if a child's death is expected, it is not always the case that he or she will die while in hospital. Many families of children facing such circumstances will opt to have their children looked after in the family home, with support from community care teams or alternatively they may receive care from a children's hospice. For these reasons it is fairly uncommon for play specialists to find that they are working with children while they actually die.

There are exceptions, of course, and the impact of the experiences of those staff and play staff who do find themselves regularly involved in working with children at such an intimate time should by no means be underestimated. The likelihood of experiencing first hand the death of a child clearly increases for those play specialists working within a ward or specialized environment where the sickest children are being treated. Clinical areas where critically ill children are looked after, including paediatric intensive care or Accident and Emergency units, may be working environments where staff experience a higher number of deaths. Similarly wards where inpatients are being treated for life-threatening illnesses, including oncology wards and cardiac units, may proportionately see more cases of patients who die in childhood.

Further to these examples are play specialists who practise within community care teams and children's hospices. Sick children and young people who have a long-term condition or whose death is expected – and their families – often opt to be cared for and eventually to die either at home, with the support of community nursing or care teams, or in a hospice. Therefore play specialists who practise within a palliative community-based or hospice-based team, for example, are likely to be more regularly and more intimately involved in the end-stage care of sick children.

Encounters with children who are facing/have faced the possibility of their own mortality

Considering, then, that death in childhood is relatively rare and not something that the majority of play specialists will witness first hand, it is perhaps both interesting and important to consider a scenario that is, by comparison, extremely common, particularly for play specialists whose work is based in a hospital setting. While play specialists here will rarely, if ever, experience being with a child as he or she dies, what they will undoubtedly encounter on a very regular basis is contact with children who through a period of illness, diagnosis of a condition or an injury will have faced and may acknowledge the possibility of their own mortality.

Work with children in this position may occur very regularly, may not always involve the sickest children and tends to have an effect upon children in the middle years of childhood and into adolescence. Younger children generally have a less developed concept of death or the risk of dying, as well as such associated factors as their understanding of a sense of time, cause and effect (Jolly 1981; Lansdown 1996). The exception to this may be found in young children who have had an experience that has allowed for an association to be created between being ill, in hospital and a subsequent death such as in the case of a fairly recent death of a loved one. It is therefore of great importance when working with sick children, even if they are now on the road to recovery, to be mindful of the impact that their experiences can have on their emotional wellbeing, especially in relation to the support they may need to cope with thoughts of death and dying.

Being able to recognize how children might behave or respond in facing the reality of their situation will be key for those involved in caring for them during their illness, including the play specialist. Some children or young people may become very withdrawn and may be fearful of discussing their thoughts or how they are feeling, either because that discussion would serve to make those feelings all the more acute, or because they are concerned about looking silly. For others the fear and shock they are experiencing may be overt or may show itself at times of stress, trauma or distress. They may appear angry or frightened, but without any particularly frightening stimulus and these strong feelings might need to be explored at a safer, calmer time.

Children who have had a pre-morbid experience, such as that outlined in the following example, may struggle with issues around death and the possibility of their own death in particular. Examples of such children may include those who have suffered a traumatic injury or been involved in a road-traffic accident. In terms of illness, children's pre-morbid experiences may well included a severe asthma attack, anaphylaxis, infections such as meningitis or pneumonia or becoming ill because of a condition such as diabetes or epilepsy. For these children the feelings of total lack of control over their bodies will probably have been frightening to the extreme. In the case of children who have a chronic condition, they may struggle with knowing that they have a condition that may cause their body to deteriorate to such an extreme level, sometimes very quickly or with little warning.

Support that can be offered to children in such situations should include a variety of age- and experience-appropriate information-sharing activities. Listening to a child's experiences and observing his or her response to these is important and serves to validate the emotional and physical response that a child has had to being injured or unwell. There is a particular value to post-procedural play, in that it can allow a child to re-visit some stressful or unpleasant aspects of his or her illness or treatment and seek answers to questions that remain around how or why the episode came about and how it was dealt with by all those caring for the child. For some children, a form of life story work, outlined in Chapter 6 of this book, may also be of value.

Jacob was 12 years old when he fell from near the top of a very tall tree. It was thought that he fell between 20 and 30 feet and as a result he sustained an open fracture of his lower leg, an injury requiring orthopaedic and plastic surgery in order for it to be repaired. Following this initial emergency treatment, the dressing over his wound needed to be changed and the wound viewed regularly. This was certainly an uncomfortable procedure, but it appeared to cause him much higher levels of stress than might otherwise have been anticipated. Despite being given adequate oral pain relief before and using Entonox gas throughout the dressing change, as the wound was exposed each time he would cry and fight the nurses and shout out 'Help me! I'm dead! I'm going to die!'

Initially it was thought that Jacob's behaviour might have been an extreme reaction to the Entonox he was using during the procedure. However, after the routine had been played out several times in the same fashion, the play specialist involved started to consider whether this might actually be an expression of Jacob's awareness that his fall could have been much more life threatening.

After discussion with the ward care team she broached the issue with him and he revealed that it was during dressing changes that he remembered – or perhaps re-lived – how frightened he had been after his fall. Added to that he was struggling with feelings of being out of control – something he had experienced at the time of his accident and was now facing again during each repeated dressing change. Discussion alone and having his feelings and this experience acknowledged seemed to calm Jacob. Things improved further when he and the play specialist planned how they were going to approach the next procedure. He opted to use less Entonox during the procedure, as this was having the effect of making him feel less in control even though it was useful in relieving his pain. When his next dressing change took place, Jacob responded well to distraction, which involved using a games console and game of his choice. He and the play specialist also communicated well throughout the procedure so that together they could identify the points where he felt most distressed. This point seemed to be that at which his leg wound was revealed as this was when his stress level peaked and he would become very emotional.

Jacob later talked about how he expected each time to see his open fracture once again and how he recalled the feelings of fear he had had at the time of the accident. At that time he believed he was going to die and so now found the repeated trauma of seeing his wound exposed to be a very real reminder of what had happened to him and how he had nearly died. Jacob's age and ability to discuss his feelings were definitely helpful in this situation. Even if children are not able to verbalize or express their feelings and fears so articulately, his experience may suggest that many children – especially those who have suffered a traumatic injury – may re-visit feelings of fear and distress, particularly during stressful experiences within the hospital setting.

If the time comes...

In the course of their work, there may be rare occasions when play specialists are asked to be involved in the care of children who are dying. At these times the play specialist will take cues from the wider multidisciplinary team as to the most appropriate or useful provision he or she can offer. However, the focus may well shift from organizing play activities to the creation of an environment that is as comfortable as possible or that contains features that are personally significant to the individual child. The play specialist's involvement with children and their families may therefore include the following:

- making sure that parents can be as comfortable as possible in the last period of time spent with their sick child, assisting them when and where possible to hold, touch or talk to their child

- the provision of particularly requested music, videos or stories

- taking photographs or giving a camera to a child's parents for this purpose

- using paint to take hand- or footprints

- providing clothes – this is especially important if a child dies in an intensive care or Accident and Emergency unit, where he or she may have been wearing few clothes. Some parents particularly wish for their child to be clothed if photographs are to be taken.

To work with a child as he or she is dying is often a highly intimate and emotive experience that many play specialists will not ever face. The death of a child, because of the challenge it can prevent professionally, personally and, more broadly speaking, sociologically, can be very stressful for all those involved in the caring. Therefore it is crucial that effective and sensitive support and supervision is on offer to members of the whole multidisciplinary team. In caring for the child who is going to die, it is important to express, at any point, if that experience is becoming overwhelming or too stressful to undertake. In the care of very ill children whose death is imminent, it might be said that an important lesson can be learned from the manual handling training so often undertaken throughout healthcare services: if the load is too heavy to lift alone, get some help in the lifting, or do not lift it at all!

Pain

All children will experience pain at some point during childhood. For some this will involve a relatively short period of acute pain, either caused by an illness or injury, or by a medical or surgical intervention, or both. A child with appendicitis, for example, will experience the abdominal pain caused by the infection in his or her abdomen, and later the post-surgical pain following a procedure to remedy the problem. Both of these experiences of pain are fairly easily relieved with adequate pain relieving medicines, although they do require careful, sensitive management and the child will need to be supported throughout his or her illness and recovery.

Other children have to live with pain caused by a chronic condition, which can persist for weeks, months or years at a time. Effectively managing this type of pain is essential for a child's sense of well-being, but can be a complex and problematic process (Dempsey 2008). Persistent chronic pain can lead to children and their parents feeling helpless and distressed, and expressing anger or frustration at those responsible for their care in hospitals, hospices or in their own homes under the care of a community team. Regardless of how children come to experience pain and how long or to which level that pain persists, it is acknowledged to be a horrible experience that needs an effective degree of recognition, response and remedy.

It is only in recent years that significant changes have taken place relating to our cultural and general beliefs about how children experience pain. Over the past 30 years medical and healthcare professionals have been challenged by the findings of research and more widely acknowledged anecdotal evidence and have accepted the following facts. First, it is acknowledged that babies and children fundamentally experience pain in a way that is very real – something that previously was not so widely accepted. Second, it is gradually being better understood that the way children experience and express what pain is like may differ very much from their adult counterparts (Aynsley-Green 2005).

When considering what the experience of pain is like for children, it is worth revisiting how children develop and understand concepts of health, illness and bodily functions (see Chapter 3) at particular ages and stages of their development. The ways that children make sense of pain and painful experiences will be influenced by their physical and cognitive development throughout childhood (Savory and Bennett 2006) and are largely seen to fall in line with the stage theory put forward by Piaget (Lansdown and Sokel 1993). That is to say that the way children assimilate information and conceptual thoughts about pain, as well as general health and illness, largely follows a logical process that moves from very concrete thinking in early childhood to more abstract thought in later childhood and adolescence. This is generally demonstrated through a shift from children being aware of what pain feels like to developing a reliable understanding of the reasons why and how pain may occur.

Over a 30-year period some fundamental or significant findings of research into children's experiences of pain have been established. These findings have had an important impact on how children are looked after in healthcare settings of all kinds and continue to push at the boundaries of how these settings respond to children's needs when they are unwell and in need of treatment. For example, it is now widely accepted that babies experience pain, a basic fact that was previously not thought to be the case. A study conducted by Taddio in 1995 (discussed in Savory and Bennett 2006) suggests that infants can suffer a significant degree of stress in response to painful stimuli, and suggested that babies who had early pain experiences showed signs of increased sensitivity to pain later on in life.

Another study, by Gaffney and Dunne (1987), found that even children as young as five years old appreciate that pain is something experienced by all people, that it is generally something that people specifically avoided, and that therefore pain is a stimulus which affects people's behaviour so as to make them deliberately avoid painful exposures. There is universal agreement throughout research that children experience and understand pain to be unpleasant from a very early point, but this particular study highlights that children's attempts or abilities to soothe, relieve or manage pain are relatively limited throughout the course of childhood. Younger children demonstrated a reliance on their adult carers for help in this regard whereas older children had developed some basic strategies for relieving or responding to their own pain, but were not able to manage its effects very effectively independently. The older children in the study also began to report that pain made them feel helpless and anxious and also were able to comment more reliably on the fact that experiencing pain goes beyond merely an unpleasant physical sensation, acknowledging that it has a psychological impact also.

Most significantly, therefore, what is gleaned from the majority of research into children's pain, generally speaking, is that regardless of age or cognitive ability, children struggle to develop effective self-initiated coping strategies independently where the experience of pain is concerned (Lansdown and Sokel 1993; Lansdown 1996). The National Service Framework for Children (Department of Health 2003) also highlights findings throughout the National Health Service that children's pain worryingly still goes under-treated in healthcare settings today. Within this document it is strongly recommended that the prevention, assessment and management of pain in infants, children and young people should be the subject of significant improvements.

These two statements clearly have significant implications for thinking about the needs of children, in various healthcare settings, who are exposed to painful procedures or treatments and who will undoubtedly require assistance in coping with those painful experiences. It means that children require staff who acknowledge what being in pain might be like for them, who will take time and effort to appropriately find out what their pain is like and who will help them to alleviate any pain that they cannot manage or bear using their own limited coping strategies. The play specialist, in this context, should be acknowledged to be a valuable and often highly effective member of the multidisciplinary team because of the practical support and advice he or she can bring to patients who are struggling to cope with pain.

Invasive medical procedures

In the average span of childhood, most children will experience a small number of invasive medical procedures even if this only consists of their routine immunization 'jabs' and the occasional sticking plaster being pulled off. Children who experience a more significant period of ill health and receive treatment for this illness in hospital are more likely to experience invasive medical procedures. The variety of procedures that children in hospital face depends very much upon the reason for their admission and the nature of their condition. However, the most common procedures faced by children in hospital today, while they are fully conscious, undoubtedly are likely to include the following:

- venepuncture (a blood sample taken by inserting a small needle into a vein)

- intravenous administration of fluid, medication, or an anaesthetic via a cannula (a small, plastic tube inserted into a vein)

- various simple injections (most commonly either a routine immunization or the injection of a local anaesthetic, for example)

- stitches to a relatively minor wound

- the application, removal or changing of a dressing on a wound

- scans (including MRI, CT, ultrasound or radioisotope scans) and X-rays.

Another issue facing children in hospital today is that it is becoming increasingly common for simple but relatively invasive procedures to be performed without sedation or anaesthetic. On the one hand, this may reduce the pressure on hospital wards as more children can be treated as outpatients without the need for admission to a ward, thus contributing to the relief of the financial squeeze facing the health services. On the other hand, however, the reality for young patients is that as more children are regularly exposed to such procedures as those outlined above, they will possibly experience a greater level of anxiety, trauma or distress as a result. Ideally, this situation requires a higher level of support and input from individuals such as play specialists, who would offer preparation for, and support during procedures. In reality, however, this support is not always fully available to balance the greater number of children facing such invasive treatment. This is of particular concern if an appropriate level of support for children and families is either not regularly provided, or at the very least not considered to be important.

Loss of physical ability and control

One of the most distressing effects of being ill for children or young people is the sense that they have lost control over their body, their level of ability or activity and ultimately their life. When specifically considering the extent to which children struggle with this, there are some significant scenarios within which anxiety caused by a lack of control can manifest itself.

The first involves the sense of loss of control caused generally by the child's experience of being ill and the ramifications of this event within his or her life. He or she will have to contend not only with the physical effects of illness and the distress caused by feeling unwell, but also with the reality that the treatment for the condition may also, at times, be unpleasant. This experience of being ill and being made well may include pain, being physically restricted or unable to get out of bed for a period of time, invasive or painful medical procedures, and great frustration over having to live with a body that does not work as well as would usually be expected. The loss of skill or ability can be very distressing for children in a variety of ways, from the purely practical (a lack of physical strength or ability or being physically tired or exhausted and having to rest for periods of time) to the downright embarrassing (loss of bladder or bowel control for example, or conditions that might affect speech or appearance).

Supporting children who are struggling with a sense of having lost some or all of their control over their bodies and their own ability to function normally can be challenging and emotive. The play specialist will plan activities with the aim of encouraging them to complete a task or master skills – whether these are new to the child or involve activities that are already familiar. This will require a certain sensitivity not to compound a child's sadness or distress by offering him or her activities that are clearly aimed at much younger or less able children. The play specialist may need to adapt activities to make them both age- and ability-appropriate. By enabling children to complete tasks and practise new or challenging skills, not only will their self-esteem receive a boost but they will, it is hoped, be able to experience an increased sense of control.

Other instances where children may develop a sense of being out of any control can result from very physical aspects of the experience. Here the child may struggle with the sense that something is being done to his or her body that is painful, uncomfortable or frightening. Children can be helped to feel more or less in control over what is happening to them depending upon whether they have been involved in any decisions that are made over procedures that are to be carried out. Other issues of importance may include whether they are restrained or held in a particular position, whether they can see what is happening during the procedure and whether they have had an adequate explanation of what will happen, as well as why and what that might feel like. These different aspects all require careful planning.

Children benefit greatly from the involvement of a play specialist in helping them to cope with the frightening feeling of being out of control. Attempting to reduce these feelings as far as possible and restore a sense of greater control needs to be a priority for the play specialist working with children facing this situation.

Being involved in making important decisions... or not

In addition to this, one of the most distressing things faced by some children may also be the feeling that many, if not all of the major decisions affecting them have been made on their behalf by adults, sometimes without adequate consultation or consideration of the child him- or herself. Increasingly in recent years, children and young people have been given greater opportunities to express an opinion about circumstances or decisions that affect them. Such recognition of the capabilities of children to participate in the processes that govern their life experiences can be linked to greater understanding of the child being the expert on his or her own life and under the UN Convention on the Rights of the Child (1990) having a right to a say in any decision by which he or she will be affected.

In the context of healthcare, the inclusion of children in important, sometimes life-changing decision-making has long been something of an ethical hot potato. There is generally found to be agreement, particularly in specific paediatric departments, that children should be given a certain degree of information about their condition and its possible treatment. There is a degree of disharmony, however, caused by the fact that every individual professional's opinion of when and how children reach a particular level of competence will differ. Cook (1999) suggests that children who are of an age and understanding to make informed decisions about their treatment should be allowed to give or withhold consent themselves for such treatment. However, genuinely allowing children to participate in such decisions to such a degree is not often observed since there are so few guidelines available to professionals working with sick children that would give a reliable indication that this appropriate level of cognitive development has been reached.

While many care teams acknowledge that children benefit from receiving information about their situation, often employing the play specialist to discuss issues of importance with children, more often than not there is little scope for genuinely seeking the child's thoughts, opinions or outright consent to a procedure or treatment regimen. In addition to this, there are also complicated legal issues that restrict the extent to which honouring children's consent (or otherwise) is feasible (Alderson 1990).

There is a sense that children – by not understanding the serious-ness of their illness or the implications of changing their treatment, for example – will make a decision for which they should not be held fully responsible, particularly if that decision in effect threatens or ends their life. Therefore by the fact that a child may well be con-sidered not to be competent enough to make important decisions, it is often the case that choices particularly round treatment are made with little or no involvement of children themselves. Studies in 1986 and 1988 by Nicholson (discussed by Lansdown 1996) perhaps offer the more helpful recommendation that consent should be sought from patients aged around 14 years, where consent is understood to mean that the patient has a full understanding of the implications of any decision having been made. Younger patients (though still from around the age of seven), having been given sound information around their treatment, should be encouraged or asked to *assent* to such treatment, that is, to show their agreement to a certain proce-dure, for example, while not being held ultimately responsible for giving it the 'go-ahead'.

The issue of consent is, in itself, enormous and hugely complicated – too complex to be properly discussed here in detail. However, it is necessary to have considered the implications for families, children and professionals of not adequately involving children in decision-making processes.

Even if children are given a certain amount of information, if they are left with a sense that they have not been asked about their feelings or appropriately listened to, this can generate anxiety, frus-tration or a sense of despair within them (Bluebond-Langner 1978; Alderson 1990). It may be the case that in order to best support children about whom significant decisions are being made, the role of the play specialist might include a mindfulness to listen actively to the child throughout any discussion that takes place around his or her condition and treatment. By attending to what the child is saying and by communicating those thoughts and opinions to others within the multidisciplinary team, the play specialist might be able to advocate to a certain degree on the child's behalf. Even if the opinion of the child doesn't dramatically affect the decision-making process in the long run, the play specialist can at least aim to ensure that his or her opinion is sought and communicated to those responsible for making difficult choices. This may also work to make sure the child knows his or her voice has been heard and, in being heard, that some degree of control has been restored to him or her.

Emotionally supporting sick children

Put in a nutshell, the most desirable and effective way of delivering good emotional support to sick children involves the provision of quality preparation before, effective distraction throughout and adequate therapeutic play on offer after traumatic, painful or difficult procedures or experiences. Such provision assumes that children will inevitably find certain aspects of their illness, treatment and care in hospital challenging and that they will not automatically be able to cope with these experiences using their own resources. Within the process of giving support, there is an understanding by the play specialist of what aspects of being ill and in hospital are stressful or unpleasant for children and why. The acceptance of these things are met with an approach seeking to help children make sense of those experiences, manage their anxiety or stress and create strategies to improve their ability to cope with the things they will face during the course of their treatment and care.

Building relationships of trust

A skill that is essential for play specialists to develop and to be able to use is the ability to connect with children – almost instantly – on first meeting and working with them, and often to then build up an important relationship if that work continues beyond a single interaction. Play specialists are often requested to work with children who are anxious and disorientated by their experience of being admitted to hospital. They may also be called on to encourage children to calm down after a procedure has already begun, especially if the child has received insufficient information about his or her treatment or a procedure or when the child is already distressed and physically resisting medical and nursing staff.

It is no mean feat for the play specialist to enter a room at this point and be expected not only to calm a child but somehow to make him or her more compliant and able to cope. However, by their training in child development, a natural ability to communicate and read children's behaviour and a 'finger on the pulse' of what children know about, find enjoyable or stimulating or what is currently fashionable (such as the latest popular TV programmes, pop stars or storybook characters), play specialists are often noted to succeed in 'reaching' and connecting with children even during times of great stress and protest.

Being able to build up this rapport with individual patients is fundamental to the success of the work carried out by play specialists (Thorp 2006). Sometimes this needs to be instant and a bond must be established very shortly after first meeting the child. Sometimes this relationship will grow over a much longer timescale of hours, days, weeks, months and, even in some cases, years. The play specialist is a valuable member of the multidisciplinary team for children because the relationship built up with patients is one based on trust – the play specialist is a reliable person who works to support children through tough or traumatic times.

Time and again, sometimes with only the minimal amount of resources and just a little bit of time, play specialists are observed to be able to remedy some very difficult or distressing situations by quickly establishing a relationship with the child and by employing strategies that distract, support or actively assist him or her in coping better. This relationship can be formed because children are able to recognize that the play specialist is there not to assist with the procedure itself, nor to restrain them or control their behaviour. When a child or young person is able to see instead that the play specialist is there to give attention fully to his or her individual needs and that the play specialist will help him or her to manage whatever frightening thing it is that he or she must face, a relationship of trust is formed that could act to underpin any further work that may follow.

Alongside trust, children also value other aspects within the relationship. Honesty is important and children often recognize that the play specialist talks to them at an appropriate level, with genuine honesty about what needs to happen to them, what they should expect and what they may well experience. Children also appreciate having someone to talk to and they know and understand that although the play specialist is an adult (as opposed to seeing him or her as a large-sized child), he or she is someone who has an understanding of children and will help to prevent them from becoming bored by providing them with lots of activities. Knowing that there is someone caring for them who has this as his or her aim and role seems to be significant, as Thorp (2006) highlights in looking at what children said when asked about about how play specialists have helped them. Josh, aged eight, nicely sums up the value placed on the relationship between play specialists and their patients: 'I would like to thank you for your support when I had the needles in my knees. You are there for me all the time and look after me' (Thorp 2006, p.21).

Planning for procedures

While the wider area of sharing information with children will be discussed in more detail in the next chapter of this book, as has previously been suggested, the broad areas of preparation and emotionally supporting children are to be viewed as not being totally separate from each other. There is inevitably and, moreover, appropriately, a crossover between the provision of good preparation for procedures and understanding that this contributes to any emotional support the play specialist can offer to sick children. When specifically considering the value of a play specialist's input prior to an invasive medical procedure or a treatment regime beginning, for example, the key feature of providing emotional support to children in this context is the planning.

Planning here should be understood to mean working collaboratively with a child or young person, giving him or her as much information as is both necessary and appropriate according to his or her age and level of cognitive development and then together creating a means by which he or she can best cope with the difficult, painful or unpleasant procedure ahead. Planning for procedures involves giving children information and then enabling them to move on to a plan of how to manage any fears or anxieties that they may hold specifically in relation to those procedures. This means that a child is not left with a lot of complex or worrying information, without later being helped to cope with the real-life event itself. To leave a child in possession of such important facts without then providing further – usually practical – support would be, at best, unhelpful and, at worst, unethical. By the means of planning and discussing with a child what will happen and how he or she will be helped to cope with that event, the child may be encouraged to become something of a partner in the decisions and details affecting his or her own treatment in hospital. This can help to restore a sense of control and ownership over his or her situation and treatment that may otherwise have been lost.

In this process, the play specialist first gives children an adequate explanation of the procedure that needs to take place and a sense of both why and how this will happen. Working with the child, the play specialist may then move fairly swiftly onto discussing what he or she intends to do with the child throughout the challenging procedure ahead to make the experience more manageable for the child. This often involves discussion around the play resources that are available and how these could be used to distract the child or to divert his or her thoughts away from the stressful situation he or she is facing. The play specialist – if appropriately trained – may discuss other relaxation or diversionary methods that could be helpful (such as guided imagery) and may explain either how this could be useful or a more definite plan of what this might involve.

One of the most important aspects of planning for medical procedures with children and young people, however, is that it can serve to teach children about their 'patient role'. Teaching about the patient role can be especially helpful for children who are particularly anxious about who does what, why, when and how during procedures and who may try to become very controlling at these times as a result. This child may want to try and dictate where he or she sits, who else is present and when or how a procedure can proceed. By the means of already being a trusted and safe member of the multidisciplinary team, the play specialist is often able to step in and – to a certain extent – re-write some of this controlling behaviour.

In this context the play specialist will aim to talk calmly to the child about the procedure itself and what it involves, who will be present and what they will be doing throughout, including the child him- or herself. This way children are not being told overtly that they must take a wholly passive role and just sit back and have a given procedure 'done to' them. Rather, they are being told what is expected from them and the rest of the people involved, as well as, it is hoped, having it communicated that 'someone else' can do the worrying on their behalf, thus allowing them to worry less. Teaching the patient role may well involve talking about positioning ('you can sit with Dad/you will sit down in the chair in the treatment room/ etc.'), setting some boundaries around behaviour ('you will need to sit very still but you can talk/shout/swear') and giving the child a positive sense of his or her own part to play in the procedure that will be carried out ('and while you have your blood test, our job is to play a game/look at a book/chat about x, y or z together').

Distraction

Although this chapter has already covered many ways in which the play specialist can support the sick child, when considering the work of the play specialist on a day-to-day basis, it is distraction that constitutes one of the most important aspects of his or her work. Alongside preparing children for medical procedures, accompanying and helping children to cope using distraction during those procedures is a mainstay of what play specialists do for a large proportion of their time.

During potentially stressful or painful experiences, and particularly during medical procedures, distraction has been accepted as being one of the most effective ways of supporting and helping children (Lansdown 1996). However, as Richard Lansdown also points out, it is important to recognize that distraction entails far more than simply flapping a toy at a child while exclaiming, 'cooee, look over there'.

Emotionally supporting sick children during procedures by the means of distraction is such a significant part of the play specialists' work that it is usually found to be an area in which the play specialist becomes highly skilled. These skills will be subtly different for all play specialists, depending on such factors as the general age of the patients with whom they usually work and the most common procedures which those patients face. A play specialist working in a healthcare centre or Outpatient department may well spend much of the working day accompanying and supporting many different children through injections, dressing changes or blood tests (venepuncture), for example, whereas a colleague based on a surgical ward may rarely assist children in coping with these procedures. Their workload much more commonly involves supporting children before they go to theatre for an operation, distracting them while they have a cannula inserted into a vein and again while their anaesthetic is administered.

Clearly the specific features of the types of work undertaken by play specialists vary according to different working environments and children who have all sorts of different needs, not to mention the often very different working styles of both individuals and whole multidisciplinary teams. However, as highly able members of the multidisciplinary team – individuals who are 'artful' in their ability to read and respond to the needs of sick children – it should be recognized that play specialists across the board possess skills in the following areas.

Communication

By means of their ability to communicate with children in very stressful circumstances, experienced play specialists use playful activities to guide and support patients, who may be frightened, distressed, angry, and who may become aggressive, in cooperating with healthcare teams so that they can cope better in the face of stressful or traumatic situations.

Working with children during medical interventions that may be traumatic and sometimes painful and which the child may find distressing can mean there is sometimes a lot of pressure on the play specialist to provide play and support for the child that is quickly effective and calming and which enables the procedure to be completed successfully. The play specialist therefore needs to be able to work in a confident and spontaneous manner, while remaining sensitive to the needs of the child throughout the duration of any invasive intervention. He or she needs to be able to communicate clearly with children who may be experiencing feelings of panic, extreme anxiety or physical pain, all of which impair their ability to concentrate, listen or process information. If the play specialist can begin to engage the child in an activity or conversation which diverts his or her attention from those feelings of fear and terror, the child can be helped to concentrate on something other than the frightening situation he or she is in. Where distraction is most effective and the child can be helped to become immersed or to focus on an alternative task, his or her feelings of anxiety and pain can be reduced.

In order to practise as well as possible, the play specialist must also develop a sense of assertiveness in communicating with his or her colleagues in the wider multidisciplinary team about the needs of children and the best ways to approach particular procedures or scenarios. Despite the fact that play specialists are often called upon once a procedure has begun and a child is already distressed, this is in no way an ideal or desirable situation for anybody involved, staff or patients. The play specialists must develop the confidence to talk with colleagues to ensure that such stressful scenarios occur less, giving way to a better approach. An improved picture would include the effective preparation of children *before* procedures begin, adequate discussion within the team around whether children would benefit from pain relief, sedation or a change in position and ongoing clarification of how best to employ the play specialist, all of which together would aim for a procedure to run as smoothly as possible.

In some more extreme circumstances the play specialist may have to be able to communicate the need for a procedure to be postponed or even aborted because it is the cause of too much distress to the child or because there is a risk of physical harm to the staff involved. Examples of such circumstances might be cases where there is a risk of a needle-stick injury when a patient will not sit still or of being kicked by a patient who has become aggressive. It can be very challenging to speak up in this manner. However, in order to advocate effectively for the child, whose needs should always be paramount, it may sometimes be necessary. Having called for a procedure to stop, the play specialist will establish a better approach to the procedure with the other professionals involved, if it is crucial to the child's diagnosis or treatment, and offer an opportunity for the child to talk over and plan for this alternative.

Approach

The approach and range of techniques employed by play specialists in order to distract patients clearly varies according to both the procedure that is being carried out and the age or ability of the patient involved. In order to work most efficiently and effectively for both staff and patients, they must be able to look at any given situation to swiftly assess the needs of the child and what needs to be provided or how people need to be positioned in order to allow that situation to progress. This assessment is often made quickly and cognitively, and may not necessarily be expressed verbally (unless there is a need to request equipment or something similar, of course). This can lead to colleagues not necessarily recognizing this particular skill of the play specialist, which constitutes a somewhat grave oversight. Having made their assessment of the situation, play specialists can respond to the individual needs of each child through a combination of sensitive and appropriate communication with the child, recognition of playthings, activities or resources that may work best in that situation, and being able to regulate and adjust the distraction that is offered through the procedure as it progresses.

As well as recognizing when and how to approach children in need of support, it is also important for the play specialist to develop a sense of confidence around when to withdraw or stop offering more and more distraction options during procedures. While most children can be helped through a stressful situation by the means of a variety of resources or activities, some children will not be able to concentrate or will simply stop communicating effectively, display-ing instead their feelings of distress by crying, shouting, screwing their eyes shut or physically resisting the invasive procedure. In such cases, rather than trying endlessly to engage the child's attention, the play specialist may well sit quietly by the child, until the procedure is completed, employing more passive strategies such as stroking, gently talking or singing to the child. If a child is feeling angry or scared and is becoming increasingly distressed, this situation cannot be positively enhanced – it will only be made worse – by the contin-uation of noisy, stimulating activities or a faceful of bubbles. This can only really act to heighten a child's sense of panic or over-stimulation and further input should therefore be avoided temporarily. Once the procedure has finished (or is aborted, should the child show signs of extreme distress) and has calmed down, the play specialist can resume some play activities so that the relationship of trust between him or her and the child can be maintained.

Knowledge and information

In order for their work to be as effective as possible, it is crucial that over time play specialists gain an extensive understanding of what is involved in specific medical interventions so that they can best sup-port children before (by means of good discussion and preparation) and throughout a procedure. This process involves getting to know, in some detail, the technical skills required by medical practitioners to complete particular procedures, discerning details such as the length of time these would usually take or what the experience might be like for the child involved. The play specialist may observe children undergoing invasive medical procedures and in doing so get a sense of the level of physical restriction that may be caused to the child or how painful or unpleasant the procedure might be to endure.

By gaining this degree of familiarity with as wide a range of medical procedures as possible, the ability of the play specialist to offer adequate, appropriate and effective support will be significantly enhanced. The process of being immersed in the procedures and treatments regularly affecting the children in their care allows play specialists to hone skills that can then be used to good effect in those specific scenarios. They will also be well equipped to prepare children for medical interventions, using information and description that is accurately based upon the observations that have been made.

By having a clear knowledge of what a particular procedure involves, play specialists begin to develop an ability to work with a child – to good effect – while simultaneously clearly understanding what the other professionals involved are doing and how the procedure itself is going. Therein lies the art of good distraction: in the play specialist's ability to give 100 per cent of his or her attention to the child who is being supported using play, while remaining well aware of the behaviour and actions of colleagues who are also involved in the procedure and being able to gauge how well the procedure itself is progressing. The play specialist may be intently focusing on and playing with the five-year-old patient while he or she undergoes a blood test, but in knowing how long a blood test usually takes, the play specialist may be able to sense – without needing to enquire – that the vein has failed or has been difficult to access. Understanding that there may be some difficulties occurring, the play specialist can also skilfully maintain the child's focus on a task, allowing his or her colleagues to continue in their efforts to obtain a blood sample.

Equipment

The range of resources utilized by play specialists in distracting children during stressful procedures is huge – endless even. However, some are more commonly used than others and may be used to make up a resource that is kept permanently in clinics, play departments or ward treatment rooms. The 'distraction box', in part, constitutes the 'tools of the trade' for play staff, allowing them to have a range of simple and effective toys, books and games at their fingertips. Broadly speaking, noisy or sparkly toys or those that are eye-catching – and by definition, distracting – are often very effective during distraction work. However, many other, sometimes quite unexpected items can also be put to good use. Books, music, board games, puppets and electronic games or games consoles are also often used to good effect. If such resources are not readily to hand or cannot be afforded by a particular healthcare setting, the power of conversation should also not be forgotten or underestimated by those aiming to calm and support children through difficult experiences. Simply asking them questions about themselves, their friends, their school, home or a favourite television show can both engage and visibly calm a child as his or her thought processes are brought back to something that is familiar and pleasurable.

Regardless of what is used, the most optimal practice should always involve settling a child into a task or activity from before the start of a procedure right through until after it has been completed. This is not always possible and it is therefore worth remembering that for a lot of procedures a child's attention may need to be diverted for only a short amount of time – in many cases this would be the few seconds needed for a needle to be inserted into a vein. The point of distraction is to bring a child's thoughts back from something that is stressful and scary to something that is altogether nicer, more manageable and less threatening, whether this is done by the use of toys and games or by means of a friendly face and an engaging conversation.

Easy access to a collection of interesting, versatile and engaging objects and activities is hugely valuable in enhancing best possible practice for the play specialist. Having the value of this resource acknowledged by other professionals can be a challenge, although it is hoped that recognition in this respect will develop as their own practice – as well as the child's ability to cope – is made easier, quicker or more effective by the involvement of the play specialist and his or her resources during clinical procedures with children.

A basic Distraction Box resource could contain:

- ✪ bubbles

- ✪ magic wand – most often used for bursting bubbles (this could be a noisy 'groan tube', sparkly glitter tube or something similar)

- ✪ simple glove or finger puppets

- ✪ small rainstick

- ✪ small wind-up/clockwork toys

- ✪ kaliedoscope or 'refraction' toys*

- ✪ board books – pop-ups, lift-the-flap or noisy button books work well

- ✪ 'search for...' books – the 'Where's Wally?' series is very popular

- ✪ rattles, noisy push-button toys or squeaky, squeezy toys

- ✪ squeezy stress ball or similar toys – to be squeezed and squashed or thrown

- ✪ a set of flash cards, which can be useful for spontaneously instigating a word or guessing game.

*Toys that require the child to look through them should be used with caution especially if the child is very anxious or nervous about the procedure s/he is facing. If children are busily concentrating on looking though a kaleidoscope and are then taken by surprise by the procedure starting when they cannot see what is happening, they may panic, physically overreact or feel that they can't trust the same thing not to happen the next time. Good communication or at least awareness that this risk is a possibility should prevent problems occurring.

To hold or not to hold? Strategic use of positioning during invasive procedures

The use of physically restraining children in order to carry out invasive procedures effectively has in recent years become something of an ethical minefield. Restraint – generally understood to mean physically holding somebody – may be deemed necessary in order to administer treatment, to obtain a necessary sample or to prevent children or young people from injuring themselves. In the context of working in a healthcare setting, for these reasons, 'restraint' is generally understood to involve an aspect of force or of something being done 'against one's will'.

Healthcare trusts are increasingly working on or working to documents known as 'clinical holding policies' which outline in detail when and how you should or should not be holding or restraining children (or patients generally) in order to carry out clinical procedures more easily. It is generally accepted that true forceful restraint should now only be used to manage the most aggressive patients or when there are simply no other options (including sedating or fully anaesthetizing a patient) in order to carry out a necessary or crucial intervention (Dartford and Gravesham NHS Trust 2007). The type of restraint that is to be used in such contexts is something in which staff would be specially trained, and certainly involves more than merely rugby tackling the patient to the ground!

On the other hand, in contrast to the issue of restraint, good positioning of patients during procedures should be understood to mean strategically holding or positioning a child or part of a child's body in order to allow a particular procedure to be carried out with as little stress or discomfort as possible. It is therefore worth considering how non-forceful holding or strategic positioning of a child during an invasive medical procedure can be used to very good effect. When it is coupled with adequate pain management and effective distraction through play, good positioning can be a key element to the success of a necessary clinical procedure.

An overarching aim of such positioning would be first so that all members of staff can complete the procedure as quickly and comfortably as possible and in such a way that the position in itself facilitates the good completion of that procedure. Another beneficial aspect of good positioning of children is that it can allow a child to be held by his or her parent or carer in a safe, secure 'cuddle', which in itself can act to reduce anxiety. Additionally, if the parent or carer can be fully involved in the process of positioning the child, and has clearly understood his or her own role in maintaining a certain position, he or she will be able to feel more positively involved as an active team player in the care of the child. While the parent or carer will need to fully understand the importance of a firm, confident hold, by playing this part he or she can provide comfort and support for the child while helping to facilitate the best possible outcome for the medical team. (Some parents do find this process challenging or distressing and therefore sensitivity by the play specialist and wider multidisciplinary team to the likelihood of such a response is important.) The play specialist can be key in helping to decide upon strategic positioning of children during medical procedures, and also in directing and supporting parents and children as they hold and are held in a certain way.

Another important function of good strategic positioning is that a child can be prevented from seeing what is involved in the procedure itself. While it is certainly the case that a minority of children need to watch the medical procedure as it is carried out on their body, the majority of children neither need to watch, nor benefit from doing so. As already mentioned above, for these children, purposeful strategic positioning, coupled with good topical pain relief/anaesthetic (especially in the case of venepuncture) and the involvement of the play specialist before and throughout the procedure, for example, can be a key aspect to an intervention being carried out successfully and completed with as little stress as possible.

Some children respond very strongly during invasive medical interventions and this in itself may necessitate a certain position being adopted either before the procedure begins (in the case of a child who is known to faint or vomit easily, for example) or may bring about a quick change in position during the procedure itself. If a child has been identified as struggling during procedures, the position he or she adopts in order to have a blood test, for example, should come into the planning that is done with him or her before this intervention begins.

Strong reactions of this nature are nearly always caused by worry, anxiety or distress in anticipation of something unpleasant or painful happening. They may also stem from a distressing experience that the child has encountered in the past, sometimes involving emergency treatment or admission. Children may experience the strong feelings of panic or terror that they recall from that time merely knowing that a certain procedure is required now. Children can be helped to cope with these feelings by a number of means including careful planning, good distraction and a lot of reassurance. If further help is required a senior play specialist – to whom the child is referred for one-to-one work – or a clinical psychologist may devise a programme of desensitization. This process can be lengthy, involving a number of carefully planned sessions, but can prove to be extremely effective.

Incentive, praise and reward

It is fairly common for children facing medical interventions or consultations to be told by their parents (and sometimes by the doctors and nurses caring for them) that they must be 'brave'. There is something of an agreement between play specialists that the use of the word 'brave' is generally best avoided with children who are facing stressful or unpleasant treatment and procedures. This is in part because obligating or demanding that a child is brave suggests a failure or reluctance to acknowledge his or her feelings of apprehension, anxiety or fear in relation to the situation. It is also because it is widely understood that bravery is exhibited in the face of something frightening. Therefore if children are told that they must be brave, they are also implicitly being given the message that something frightening lies ahead of them, and this can heighten a sense of fear or apprehension.

Following the completion of a difficult or unpleasant procedure is a more suitable time within which to praise a child for how well he or she has coped and to commend the child on how brave he or she has been. To demand bravery from an already anxious child is unreasonable and has the potential to jeopardize the successful completion of the procedure by raising his or her sense of fear or apprehension. To draw attention to how brave the child was after he or she has indeed exhibited bravery in the face of a frightening or difficult experience is much more appropriate and may well boost a child's self-esteem and self-confidence into the bargain.

When considering the use of rewards and incentives for children – generally in life as well as more specifically when they are unwell – it is perhaps useful to acknowledge that there is a difference between bribing children to behave well and offering them an incentive to achieve a goal or to aim for a particular outcome. Bribing a child would involve giving them something desirable (sweets, chocolate, allowing them to watch TV or play on a games console) and then telling them they must behave a certain way ('Have these crisps: *now be good!*'). Offering an incentive, on the other hand, involves setting a realistic aim or a goal with a child and letting the child know clearly that if that goal or aim is achieved then he or she will receive a reward or some recognition for his or her effort ('When you have had your dressing changed, then we can play a game on the X-Box').

Understanding and being able to explain this fundamental difference in approaches to encouraging compliance is key to the work of the play specialist, who may often be jovially accused of bribing children so that they will behave in a certain manner. Being able to demonstrate that rather than bribing a child – which does little either to achieve a set goal or to boost the child's sense of achievement – the best approach is always to offer an incentive. This approach not only boosts self-esteem, but also encourages children to comply with further treatment should they require it in the future.

Praise and rewards of varying types including stickers, certificates and small prizes can also have a positive effect on children's self-esteem or can reinforce their sense of achievement following a difficult procedure or the completion of a course of treatment. This type of reward is regularly used in healthcare settings and can be particularly effective with toddlers and young children. However, it is important always to reward children's effort and not only their achievements. If a reward is given it must be done so in recognition of the child's attempts to comply and cooperate and all he or she has endured regardless of whether the outcome of the procedure was entirely successful (Lansdown 1996).

Star or sticker charts are often employed to encourage compliance in young children. Those who have gained a desired quantity of stickers will usually be given a prize or treat as a reward for their good behaviour. This reward system could have the aim of persuading children to take regular medicines, to have creams applied or dressings changed, to eat or drink certain quantities of food or drink or to cooperate during examinations or therapy sessions. Whatever the desired outcome, the use of a sticker chart can be very effective. It must, however, only be used where the desirable behaviour is easily achievable and where the goal is clearly set out to the child.

The danger with reward systems of this nature is that the behaviour is for one reason or other simply not possible for the child at this point in time, making it impossible for children to gain rewards, and the result will therefore be that the desired boost to self-esteem will be lost or even destroyed. It can also present a difficulty if the system of gaining stickers is just too complex – a system where stickers are given for good behaviour but withdrawn for less desirable behaviour, for example. In such cases, children will become disheartened very early in the process, stop cooperating or stop trying to behave in the desired way. This in turn could make the child feel as if he or she has failed which will not improve the situation that the reward system had set out to remedy. Sticker charts can be a simple and effective first step in gently changing a child's behaviour or habits. In spite of their simplicity, they should still be used with clear boundaries and, in some instances, even with a degree of caution.

In some healthcare settings, hospital wards or departments, the role and work of the play specialist remains a little-understood and often under-used resource. However, an exploration of the emotional needs of sick children and due consideration of the breadth of the play specialist's role in this context highlights how significant that role can be in enhancing a child's ability to understand and cope with the stressful or unpleasant things encountered during a period of illness and treatment.

If play specialists are accepted as regular and respected members of multidisciplinary teams, over time and largely by the means of practical demonstration, their wealth of skills and knowledge will be recognized and valued by colleagues and patients alike. By demonstrating an ability to communicate well with both patients and colleagues, the possession of a sound knowledge of the procedures within which he or she will regularly be involved and having a good stock of useful resources to hand, the play specialist should gain recognition as being an asset to the teams in which he or she works.

By their 'artful' ability to meet, greet and support children through some of their toughest times play specialists are able to make a genuine difference to them. Play specialists' work in this area, outlined in Figure 5.1, can meet many needs – enabling children, families and professionals to work together for the benefit of the child requiring medical treatment or hospital care. The support and interventions they bring to a wide range of situations are valuable not only to those children and their families who are helped to cope in the face of stressful or distressing experiences, but also to the range of professionals whose work can be made a little easier by their patients' improved ability to cope.

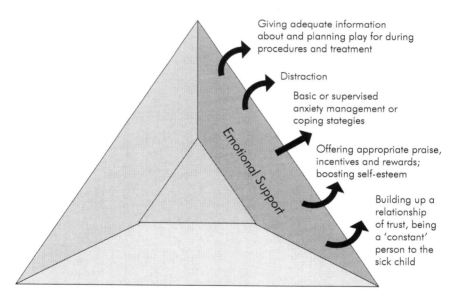

Giving adequate information about and planning play for during procedures and treatment

Distraction

Basic or supervised anxiety management or coping stategies

Offering appropriate praise, incentives and rewards; boosting self-esteem

Building up a relationship of trust, being a 'constant' person to the sick child

Emotional Support

Figure 5.1 Emotionally supporting sick children

6

Imparting Information

Children's anxieties may seem fanciful, but they are none the less real to the child, and an opportunity should be taken to talk to the child about his forthcoming treatment and, as far as possible within the limits of his understanding, to explain to him what is involved. (Platt 1959, p.28)

The key to coping

The importance of suitable and adequate preparation of children coming into hospital was a major theme of Harry Platt's 1959 report on the welfare of children in hospital, one to which he returned again and again throughout his observations and recommendations. Platt was unequivocal in his conviction that 'the risk that any child will be disturbed by hospital admission can be reduced by suitable preparation of both parents and children' (Platt 1959, p.11).

James Robertson, though in agreement that children should be offered a certain degree of information about any forthcoming hospital admission, was more cautious in his observations, believing that children much under about the age of eight years were not able to take on such information in any useful way (Robertson 1970). In spite of this, he was emphatic about the need for children to receive simple and truthful explanations for why they were to be admitted to hospital, and that they should certainly not be given false information or assurances that could not be delivered. Robertson recognized that the relationship of trust between parent and child needed as far as possible to be preserved and that this preservation was at risk as soon as parents tried or were encouraged – wrongly – to tell their children that they would not encounter pain or any unpleasant sensations or experiences during their hospital treatment, for example.

In spite of some of his misgivings about preparing children for hospitalization, Robertson did, however, like Platt, bring the issue of preparing and sharing information with children about their health, illness, treatment and possible need for hospital treatment into the mindset of those concerned with the care and treatment of sick children and young people. These are two of the major threads of work, with their concern around the specific needs of children when they are unwell and in hospital, that contributed significantly to the weaving together of a role we now recognize as being that of the play specialist.

And so it is that the third central aspect of the play specialist's role is that of giving information to children and young people, not just about their admission to hospital, but also a wide variety of topics that can enlighten them on what may happen to them because of a particular condition or during a course of treatment. The broad aim of the play specialist here is to aid the development of an appropriate level of understanding about their situation, and in doing so to foster effective coping strategies. More specifically the aim may be to enable a child to face the stress or challenge of undergoing an invasive procedure, the completion of which can be brought about in as straightforward a manner as possible. It is these aims, broad and specific in their nature, yet both concerned with enhancing a child's ability to understand and cope with his or her situation, that will be explored in this section.

Caution: jargon ahead!

Information sharing with children and young people by play specialists is most commonly referred to simply as 'preparation'. To those very familiar with the work of hospital play professionals the meaning of this term would be instantly understood. However, to any other person this could be considered as being a form of medical jargon, similar to some of those discussed in the previous section of this book. This is similar to discussing the emotional support of children simply as 'distraction' – a term that gives relatively little away to patients and colleagues who may not be familiar with hospital play jargon about what that work fully involves.

It is also worth considering how describing such a significant area of the play specialist's role simply by using the term 'preparation' serves to diminish the complexity of this whole area because, as an expression, it gives away almost no detail of what this aspect of their work involves. The term 'preparation' – and even more so, its commonly used abbreviation of simply 'prep' – can be one that is highly value-laden, in that it encompasses many and varied aspects of information sharing. To the casual observer, uninformed colleague or to parents of a sick child, however, it is also vague in the extreme. When used alone with no supporting explanation offered, the expression 'preparation' tells the listener very little – even nothing – about this important area of the play specialist's work.

In an environment where play staff often have to fight to get the value of their work recognized or appreciated by those with whom they work, there is a need then to exercise some caution when describing the scope of play work in healthcare settings by the use of so simple a term, without necessarily offering an adequate explanation of what it means. Perhaps it is worth considering what play specialists mean when they talk of 'preparation'? What are the processes (thought and planning) that go into that area of work? Does describing such an important aspect of the play specialist's work often require a little more elaboration in order to reflect the knowledge and skill that is involved in that work?

When play specialists discuss offering or carrying out 'preparation' with patients, generally they are referring to a time specifically set aside for exchanging, sharing and giving information to children, young people and also their parents and sometimes siblings about a particular issue, treatment or procedure. This may be carried out at their bedside, in an Outpatient clinic, before or after their admission to hospital, in the ward playroom or even in their own home. This session may involve the use of resources specifically designed for the purpose of increasing a child's knowledge about an area of his or her health, illness or treatment. It may equally involve, although to a somewhat limited degree, an element of free play with 'small world' figures, dolls, puppets or actual medical equipment.

However, this play often differs from the freely accessed normalizing play on offer because within the boundaries of a specific 'preparation' session, this apparently 'free' play may actually contain some fairly guided elements, brought by the play specialist whose aim it is to further a child's understanding in a particular area. Play specialists approach the preparation of children having themselves gained as full an understanding as possible of that child's situation, condition and any treatment he or she may require. With this knowledge in place, the play specialist can confidently and skilfully adapt the preparation work offered, and select the most suitable resources or methods to ensure that that child in turn receives reliable, honest and appropriate information.

When the term 'preparation' is so commonly used as an umbrella explanation for a considerable chunk of the play specialist's work, it belies the complex planning and delivery processes that often go into making sure children and young people understand and cope as well as possible on their journey through the course of a period of illness, treatment and recovery. Play specialists therefore need to ensure that they are clear with colleagues, parents and even themselves about what they mean and what is involved in the process that is 'preparation'.

Elements that will determine the effectiveness of preparation

Play specialists gaining and retaining the right information

Clearly, if the information given to children is going to be at all helpful, it is important that it is both accurate in its content and confidently delivered. For this reason play specialists themselves must be in possession of accurate and detailed information in the first place. Therefore they have a responsibility to find out as much as they can about the clinical areas within which they work, the conditions with which their patients most commonly present, and the procedures and treatments most often undergone by patients as well as what these involve and the reasons why they are carried out. Should a child require preparation for a procedure or treatment with which the play specialist is unfamiliar, time must be taken to find out all the necessary information so that this can be shared with the child. It could even be suggested that to attempt to prepare a child if this 'finding out' has not been adequately done, is unprofessional or irresponsible. A confident, knowledgeable approach acts to instil trust and reliability within the relationship between play specialists, children and their families. Having sought and retained the right information is an important key to the overall effectiveness of any preparation on offer.

Further to this important starting point, the following issues demand some consideration when preparation is thought to be necessary since they all – individually and in combination – have the potential to guide the planning and delivery of preparation work with sick children and to influence the outcome or effectiveness of such work.

Age and developmental stage

It would be very simple to suggest – and indeed to believe – that the younger the child, the less likely it is for him or her to realistically take in or respond appropriately to any preparation he or she might receive for medical treatment or procedures. However, age is not necessarily a straightforward area around which to make such judgements. There are a great many other variables that will affect a child's readiness or ability to benefit from preparation. Younger children tend to be thought of as less able to benefit from preparation because they are, generally speaking, less skilled at verbal communication including asking questions and the expression of complex emotions. They generally have a more basic and potentially more muddled understanding of bodily functions and the causes and effects of illness, and it is not thought necessary to involve them in formal or planned preparation sessions prior to treatment (Lansdown 1996).

Chronological age alone however – as has previously been discussed in a number of contexts – does not necessarily follow a linear or logical correlation to a child's cognitive development or physical ability. Children develop in their thoughts and ability to take on new information as individually as they do in appearance or physical stature. Despite their relative inability to verbalize complex issues, children often take in and understand far more than they are able to say at an early age. The ability of the play specialist lies in the skills that will enable his or her assessment of each individual child's need for preparation in the face of hospitalization or invasive procedures. This assessment is often made by the means of a combined instinctive and theoretical knowledge of children and will take into account their level of cognitive ability, the need to give children – even those who are very young – some meaningful explanation of what they are experiencing and why, and also to pick up on cues the child may be giving that he or she needs to know more. The skill of the play specialist will be in judging when it is necessary to offer information to children and to be able to determine the most appropriate approach to the individual child according to his or her particular circumstances or needs.

Taking this into account, however, a very generalized approach to preparing children for invasive treatment or procedures that is based solely on age is outlined in the NAHPS *Let's Play* booklet by Weiss (1987). An adapted version, suggesting the approach and methods that can and should be used at each given age, is presented in Table 6.1.

It is possible that where very young children are concerned, it is not so much a question of whether there is a need for preparation, but that there is a need to reconsider the method or approach to using play in order to encourage and enable small children to take on new or complex information. While preparation is often delivered as a planned and structured session in which children are shown and told about the things that are relevant to their lives or experiences, with younger children, perhaps, it can be more powerful to include 'relevant' play objects or characters in an environment where they can play freely and become acclimatized to those features. These could include such things as dolls with lines or dressings already in place as well as medical equipment such as syringes and stethoscopes. (For this reason, 'hospital play' is included as one of the methods of offering preparation to children.)

By partly observing and partly being an active player in the child's active, imaginative play, the play specialist might be able to impart some sense of why these objects or characters are significant to the child him- or herself. The play specialist could story-tell about the character of the doll who faces a similar situation to the young child with whom he or she is working. The play specialist may then return to this story-telling in order to remind the child of the things encountered in their play activities in future preparation work if this is deemed to be appropriate.

Table 6.1 Age-determined preparation: aims and methods

Age of child	Who needs preparing?	What do they need to know?	What resources could be used?
0–12 months	Parents; older siblings	What is going to happen? Why? How? What will this be like for the child?	Photographs can be very helpful where deemed suitable; body maps or diagrams can help parents understand conditions and treatments.
1–3 years	Parents; individual child's needs to be assessed; older siblings	What is going to happen? Why? How? By what means will the child be helped to cope?	Storybooks and basic photo books (frequently used within pre-admission clinics) can be helpful as can hospital/ward visits prior to admission. Dolls can be useful to young children encouraging hospital play and expression of feelings/experiences.
3–6 years	Children; parents; older siblings	What is going to happen? Why? How? What will this be like for the child? What is the child's/play specialist's role?	Preparation using dolls or models; hospital 'free' play including dressing-up and role play; photographs and ward visits during pre-admission clinics; conversation around feelings, worries and planning for procedures.

Table 6.1 cont.

Age of child	Who needs preparing?	What do they need to know?	What resources could be used?
7–11 years	Children; parents; siblings	What is going to happen? Why? How? What will this be like for the child? What is the child's/play specialist's role?	Preparation using dolls or models; photographs and ward visits during pre-admission clinics; conversation around feelings, worries and planning for procedures.
12 years +	Children; parents; siblings	What is going to happen? Why? How? What will this be like for them? Expectations or boundaries around behaviour? What is their/the play specialist's role?	Photographs and a ward visit could be useful if admission is planned; body maps or diagrams can help teenagers understand conditions and treatments. Dolls can be used to show what a blood test or similar procedure involves, if child is comfortable with their use; peer support can be powerful where appropriate; conversation around feelings, worries and planning for procedures.

Previous experiences of medical interventions or being in hospital

The effects of hospitalization on children have previously been identified as potentially different according to whether those children are acutely ill or whether they have a long-term or chronic condition. The same can be said for considering the preparation needs of children according to any experiences they may previously have had.

Children's previous experiences – whether these are very recent or relatively historical – can be very significant in determining how well (or otherwise) children will cope when faced with difficult situations. If a child's only experiences of healthcare settings have been traumatic and painful, then he or she may well come to expect only this, and may therefore react with protest, panic or fear each new time. Distressing experiences may come to be the root of phobias or behavioural problems such as non-compliance or anticipatory anxiety should a child face a similar situation in the future.

A child's medical history will also determine the type and level of information that will be helpful to him or her. The play specialist may work with one patient who has no previous hospital experience, needing to reassure and inform that child about the hospital environment and different roles of the staff caring for hiim or her as well as any surgical or invasive medical procedure he or she must undergo. The next patient, however, may be a child who had experienced many hospital admissions, undergone multiple interventions and knows some of the staff on first-name terms! The method of preparing or sharing information with these two patients will clearly be very different, as their needs are so very different. Part of the play specialist's role is to be able to determine the different types and levels of information that will be needed by children taking into account a variety of different factors, not least any previous experiences they have had and how they reacted to these experiences.

The emotional wellbeing of the child's parents

Coping with the practical and emotional effects of having a sick child can be a difficult and draining experience for parents. They may experience feelings of guilt, extreme anxiety and worry, helplessness and an overwhelming sense of having lost control over the decisions to be made over their child's care and general wellbeing. Parents under stress have reported feelings of not being able to function normally, to make decisions effectively nor to respond to their child's needs or condition as they usually would (Cook 1999). Children, in turn, can be highly attuned to and aware of the strong, sometimes negative emotions that may run high around them and that may be being experienced by their parents or close family members.

This is significant when considering how the emotional wellbeing of parents might determine the effectiveness of any preparation offered to children, because as Dempsey (2008, p.26) observes, 'how the parent copes…affects how the child copes'. It is likely, therefore, that if a parent is struggling with the stress and strain of his or her child's condition and feeling unable to cope or take on new or complex information, the child may also struggle and as a result, may not benefit fully from any preparation or information sharing that is offered by the play specialist. Children, in sensing and sharing their parents' distress or worry, may not be able to retain or effectively use the information they are given.

In more extreme cases, parental anxiety or fear may cause them to block or avoid allowing information to be shared with their children around their condition or its treatment.

Timing

In thinking about the best time to prepare children for surgery or particular procedures, there is a fine balance to be struck between giving them enough time to take on new information, ask questions and play through all they have heard or learnt, while not allowing too much time as this might allow for anxiety to grow, or for them to begin fantasizing over what they have been told. This balance is something that will be subtly different for individual children and something that the play specialist will need to gauge while getting to know them, and by taking into account all of the above issues.

As a general rule, however, it is suggested that children facing surgery should be told in appropriate detail what is going to happen to them towards the end of the day before scheduled morning operations, and during the morning of the day if they are on the afternoon surgery list (Weiss 1987). When preparing children for blood tests, if a topical anaesthetic cream such as EMLA or Ametop is used, it is logical that the 30 minutes required for this to take effect should be used by the play specialist to talk to the child about what will happen and why, and to discuss the patient role and plan distraction activities. Where this topical pain relief is not used, the play specialist may need to ensure that adequate time is made available for this preparation and planning to still go ahead.

Preparation will need a different approach and requires a different focus in the following situations:

- when a child's admission is planned

- when a child's admission is not planned, especially if it is an emergency admission

- when preparation is offered for a specific procedure (rather than a general admission)

- when preparation is given for procedures or treatments that are painful or unpleasant

- when preparation is given for diagnostic tests where the outcome is uncertain (this scenario could include increased parental stress, may follow an emergency admission and there may be less certainty over what/ how much information to give).

The aims in preparing children for treatment or procedures

Therefore, having taken into account the variables outlined above and having made an informed decision around how much information to share with a child, as well as how much detail this information should contain, the play specialist's main aims in offering preparation to children or young people can be outlined as follows:

- to familiarize children and families with healthcare settings, staff, treatments or procedures

- to eliminate and put right any fantasies and misconceptions the child may have

- to help children cope by giving them reliable honest and factual information so that they will know and understand what will happen, why and when

- to instil confidence in children and their parents, helping them to feel more relaxed

- to help children face, express or cope with fear or anxiety

- to reduce post-procedural stress or trauma through play and talking.

The NAHPS Guidelines for Professional Practice, produced in 2002 in order to support the practical and clinical work of play specialists, also suggests three further aims of preparation through play. The first two can be seen as being quite broad in their intention of reducing the psychological effects of a hospital admission both in the short and long term and also of speeding a child's recovery. NAHPS (2002) also state the importance of offering high quality preparation as a means through which informed consent to treatment, examination or medical intervention can be given.

What resources do play specialists use for preparation?

Play specialists use a wide range of resources with which to talk to children and their parents about conditions, hospital treatment and medical procedures. Broadly speaking these are usually produced by play staff themselves, partly because that way they can include details that may be specific to a particular hospital, ward, department or medical team. A further reason why the production of preparation resources is in the hands of individual play specialists is that they are rarely available to purchase by any other means. With the exception of a few dolls or bears that can be used to demonstrate blood tests and the insertion of lines, and illustrate some basic issues of anatomy, the design and manufacture of resources is the responsibility of play specialists and their colleagues, having identified the needs of the children in their care. With that in mind, the methods and resources most often used by play specialists to prepare or give information includes the following.

Talking, listening and answering questions

Conversation is the primary method of preparing children for new experiences. Talking about new situations before and around the time that they arise is done by all those involved in the care of children, whether that care is based at home (parents, close family, friends, teachers) or in a variety of healthcare settings (doctors, nurses, healthcare assistants and play staff). The key consideration for play specialists, however, is to ensure that when children are allowed to explore complicated issues or to express fears or worries, those conversations deliver adequate, consistent, honest and reliable information that is appropriate to their age or level of cognitive development.

Dolls

A mainstay of preparation work carried out by the hospital play specialist involves using dolls to talk about and sometimes to demonstrate invasive procedures and treatments. Although it is possible to purchase a handful of specially adapted dolls for this purpose, the majority of those used by play specialists have been made by play departments themselves, by adapting mass-produced dolls for a variety of purposes. The most common adaptation that is made to these dolls is the insertion of a small bag of fluid (a 'drip' bag, usually used for intravenous treatment) so that it can be used to demonstrate to children what venepuncture is like. By adding red food colouring to the fluid inside, inserting the bag into an arm or foot of a soft-bodied doll and positioning the resealable bung of the drip bag in the back of the doll's hand, arm or foot (i.e. the most common sites from which a blood sample may be taken) the play specialist can use a real needle and syringe to demonstrate taking a 'blood' sample from the doll. On the assumption that the dolls generally used by play specialists are fairly large, it is usually the case that real hospital equipment can be used on them during preparation sessions. In this respect, preparation using dolls can also be seen to constitute a form of hospital play that can allow children to explore and re-visit some of the elements experienced or witnessed during their hospital admission.

The use of dolls with sick children is often especially effective because they can provide the means to talk about difficult emotions and worries in a non-direct way. Children may well choose to play through some of their difficult experiences either by seeming to project the things they have faced themselves onto the character of the doll or by telling the doll directly what has happened to them.

Equally the play specialist, by the use of a doll, may able to explore difficult or strong emotions with children in relation to medical procedures. They may 'story tell' or describe the procedure that the doll — and the child him- or herself — is facing, while asking at various key points how the doll is feeling (such as when her anaesthetic cream is applied over a vein, when the needle is used to access a vein and after the procedure has finished). This can give the play specialist some indication of the strong feelings with which the child him- or herself may be trying to cope and can give way to planning for the child's own forthcoming procedure or talking about how these feelings can best be managed.

Models

In addition to using dolls for a variety of preparation activities, play specialists also utilize models for some of the work required. The types of models used, broadly speaking, include small world models plus the use of real hospital equipment or artefacts. While real objects are also often used alongside a doll or are featured in photograph books, they are sometimes just useful to show to children so that they can be handled, explored and discussed. An example of the types of real-life 'models' or equipment that could be valuable would be nasogastric tubes and intravenous lines, including cannulas, or facial jigs moulded to be worn by a child undergoing radiotherapy.

Small world models used in addition to general hospital play sets (such as those produced by Playmobil or the Early Learning Centre's 'Happy Land' set), like specially adapted dolls, are often produced by play specialists themselves in the absence of commercially produced models. These often depict experiences of having a variety of scans, most commonly MRI or CT scans, and can allow the play specialist to show children how a certain procedure will progress, while giving a certain sense of scale. For example, when using a model of an MRI scanner, with a small figure to represent the patient, a child will see how individuals travel right inside the scanner in order for the procedure to be carried out. The child is then able to ask questions and raise their concerns or fears having watched a representation of the procedure in model form.

Models can also be useful because essentially they allow children to explore issues and emotions through small world play within which they can practise a sense of mastery and control. By being able to be the boss (perhaps 'the doctor' or simply the decision-maker), children are able to act out or explore the situations they face and to make some sense of them (Young 2008). They are also enabled through small world play to make decisions at a time when a lot of important decisions are made by the adults involved in their care, but without their consent or consultation.

Books and photographs

There is a wealth of books in production that aim to introduce children to ideas and details of what the experience of going to the doctor's, dentist's or hospital might be like. Some of these books are very good and may successfully give children a first impression of these experiences, they do tend to follow a predictable storyline, which involves a well child being admitted to hospital for a simple, routine operation. Although these books may be useful when they are used in community settings such as nurseries, schools and the home environment, they are of little relative value for sick children who are admitted to hospital for any other reason or in any other circumstances, or for children who have a chronic, life-threatening or life-limiting illness and as such, they do little to reflect these real-life experiences of being unwell or their treatment in hospital.

For this reason, many play specialists respond to the needs of the children with whom they work by producing their own written and pictorial guides. These may be used to prepare children specifically for a forthcoming admission to hospital, using words and pictures (often photographs of the actual ward and staff where a child will be staying) and make up some of the resources most often used during pre-admission clinics. Alternatively they may be used to introduce children to invasive procedures, such as blood tests, allergy testing, scans of various kinds, or intravenous treatment. Books used for this purpose may contain photographs or picture illustrations, but also aim to explain simply and clearly what procedure a child must undergo as well as the reason for this intervention and an explanation of what will happen, who will be present and aspects of what constitutes the child's 'patient role'. They may also outline to the child the extent to which he or she can make active choices around the procedure (choosing who accompanies him or her and what to play with as distraction, for example) and will also be clear where the child's ability to make choices is minimal. This is not necessarily written overtly, but the use of positive language should mean that the message implicitly received by the child is that the procedure will go ahead.

Photographs can be especially powerful to children, especially if they are unfamiliar with the hospital environment. Photo-books must be regularly updated, however, as children will expect the pictures to be accurate and some children may be thrown if key elements of the images featured (such as ward décor or staff uniforms) have changed when they are admitted to hospital.

'Life story' work

The term 'life story work' is taken from the work undertaken mainly with children who are 'looked after' – that is, fostered or in local authority care of some sort – or who have been adopted. This type of work is usually embarked on with these particular children to explore their personal life histories and also to approach some of the scenarios and issues that have led them to have been taken into care and the reasons why life-changing decisions were made on their behalf. While this very specific type of work is not undertaken by play specialists, the power of life story work lies in that gathering together facts about the significant issues affecting a child's life can help the child begin to accept the past and move forward into the future in possession of this knowledge. It also provides a very helpful, structured approach to information sharing with children and young people (Ryan and Walker 2003). Therefore some of the elements of why life story work is valuable for children can be 'borrowed' by those working with sick children, including play specialists who may consider it appropriate to help a child make sense of a difficult diagnosis, chronic illness or life-changing decision that is made with his or her wellbeing at its core. An important essence of life story work is that it tells a child's story from its beginning (or even before) and puts into context how a child has come to be where he or she is today.

For children who have been ill for some time and are perhaps struggling to make sense of their situation, to use activities or techniques that are similar to life story work in that essence can be very powerful. Activities of this nature allow children to participate in telling their own story, to present facts alongside their own emotional responses and experiences of being ill, and also allow them to ask hard, sometimes almost unanswerable questions ('Why do *I* have CF and not my brother...?') and explore possible answers to these questions. Life story-type work may take the form of creating a scrapbook with children meaning that they end up with their own 'resource' that contains valuable information about their life, condition and experiences and which also allows them to return to this resource again and again, adding more information or details as required.

Information to take away

While they are responsible for the creation of a wealth of information that is used both with children while they are inpatients and also those who are due to be admitted to hospital in the future, play specialists may also be involved in the process of producing information for children and their parents to take home with them from outpatient appointments or when they are discharged from hospital. This may constitute information that is produced specifically for children, to tell them in child-friendly terms more about their condition or its treatment. Alternatively it may take the form of information that is suitable for the whole family, about which the play specialist has been consulted so as to ensure that the details that might be included in preparation sessions is appropriately included.

Free play

The majority of the preparation work undertaken by play specialists is both adult-led and fairly structured as it tends to have a specific purpose and planned outcome – that is, to explain details of medical interventions and treatment to children in order to help them cope as well as possible with those experiences. However, it is also possible to consider certain aspects of a child's free play, particularly hospital play, as being of value in helping him or her to take on, process and consolidate new or complex information about what it means to be unwell and made better. Hospital play has previously been looked at in some detail in Chapter 4 of this book. However, as a less structured yet hospital-focused activity its value can lie in the opportunities it presents for children to choose and motivate their own activities in relation to areas they wish to explore or 'play out'. The part played by the play specialist should a child opt to take part in free play using hospital-themed toys and props (in addition to the initial provision of those things, of course) may be purely to observe the child at play and to notice his or her behaviour and the narration in which he or she is engaged while playing.

Two preparation types

It is clear then that children require different types of information or reassurance at different times, depending on quite a number of different factors, including the environment in which they are seen or being looked after and whether any invasive procedures are to take place. In considering styles of preparation, there are two main types of preparation that are offered to children and young people by play specialists, the delivery methods and broad aims of which are distinct from one another.

Broad preparation

The what, why, and who approach

The first type of preparation that children are seen to receive for the experience of going to hospital could be described as being general or oblique in its nature. While this broad type of preparation is un-doubtedly provided by play specialists – in ways that will shortly be discussed in more detail – information of a very general nature about what hospitals are, why they exist and the kind of people who work there will begin to be passed to children within a wide range of settings from a very early age. Children learn from a vast variety of sources and in many different ways. It is therefore very likely that they will learn something – however rudimentary – about the experiences of being ill, being looked after, seeing a doctor or nurse, or being seen in or admitted to hospital, in their own home, their pre-schools, toddler groups and from their parents, close family members, other carers or indeed from other children themselves.

There are also many books available for young children that tell stories of children's significant 'first experiences', which often give a first look at seeing the doctor (or dentist) or going into hospital, or both. Similarly children's television programmes regularly look at what it is like to be ill, to need to see a doctor or to go to hos-pital. While children may appear to be passive observers of such programmes they undoubtedly take in and process a lot of the infor-mation they witness via the television screen.

Children also learn a lot from each other and from their parents, relatives and carers. They will pick up signals, particularly from their parents or siblings, about whether healthcare centres and hospitals are good places or whether their response to them should be one of caution or fear. There can also be no more powerful a statement to a child than the experience of a much-loved grandparent, relative or even a pet going into hospital (or in the case of the pet, to see the vet!) and perhaps never returning home again. Children could easily – and often do – make a marked association between hospitals and death. This is where the informal, broad-scale preparation or gleaning of information about illness, doctors, nurses, hospitals and all manner of related issues can become problematic or at the least, prove itself to be limited by its subjective nature. In the big wide world, children observe, overhear, misunderstand and can become entrenched in believing some of the many facts, figures or ideas about what hospitals are and what happens to you when you are there. Some of these ideas may be very accurately understood while others may lead to significant misunderstandings about the sorts of things that might happen to you if you become unwell and need to be cared for in hospital.

While some of the more accurate resources available for children aim to give them an idea of what a 'first experience' of going to hospital or to see the doctor might be like, they are not always entirely helpful as they only give an account of one type of scenario and are usually based – understandably so – around something very predictable and relatively safe. While this is probably better than there being no resources whatsoever, an account of Jim being hospitalized to have his tonsils removed does little to prepare a child for his or her first experience of breaking a bone and being treated in an Accident and Emergency department, for example. The two experiences are very different, but the book – while limited in its helpfulness – does at the very least introduce children to some basic and fairly manageable facts about hospitals. In spite of those limitations, these facts probably constitute the foundation knowledge that could be seen as the aim of all of this broad, general and oblique type of preparation in its attempt to establish the following:

- *What* are hospitals? (Big buildings where you go, when you are not well)

- *Why* do you go there? (To be made better)

- *What* happens when you get there? (You see a doctor or a nurse, then 'something' happens (medicine, X-ray, operation) and then you will get better)

- *Who* will you meet there? (Doctors, nurses, other patients, other members of staff, and your parent(s), of course).

While it may be something of a sweeping statement, it is perhaps not unreasonable to suggest that most, if not all children could re-count the basic facts about hospitals as outlined above by some time around their fifth birthday. Some of this knowledge will be in place purely because they have access to television or reading resources or because they have had some conversational preparation with parents, carers, friends or pre-school teachers that has been helpful in their grasp of what hospitals are like.

This broad type of preparation also plays a major part in the work of play specialists who help children find out and understand more about an admission to hospital. This may be during the play specialist's initial dealings with a family after they have been admit-ted to a ward for treatment or it may form a significant part of a pre-admission clinic or programme in advance of an admission that is due to take place relatively shortly in the future.

On first meeting children and their families, to a greater or lesser extent, the play specialist will aim to establish what children under-stand about their admission, whether they understand why they are there and ensure that they are coping with an environment and the variety of staff that may seem very new and overwhelming. With this as a base, more information can be offered to children, as required, to enable them to cope as well as possible with their experience of being unwell and any treatment they receive.

Pre-admission programmes

One of the ways in which this broad type of preparation is offered to children and their parents, specifically by play specialists, is through organized pre-admission clinics or programmes, which families are invited to attend prior to a planned admission to hospital. These pre-admission services themselves might be seen to fall into two main types. The first of these involves sharing fairly general information with a group of children who all attend a pre-admission session together, whereas in the second example the play specialist sees children on a one-to-one basis in a pre-admission clinic setting, giving them information that is much more specific to their individual circumstances. This latter example will be discussed later in this chapter.

The first example of a pre-admission programme, however, aims to ensure that children due to be admitted to hospital for a planned, usually surgical procedure are in possession of the basic information about hospitals, so that they will cope as well as possible with the prospect of being cared for in that, thus far, alien environment. Sometimes given a child-friendly name such as 'Saturday Club' (if held on a Saturday morning, for example), these events invite a number of children to attend all together, anywhere from one to four weeks before their admission takes place. They generally seek to introduce and acclimatize children to the strangeness of the hospital environment through activities, storytelling and ward or hospital tours.

This type of pre-admission clinic exists to reinforce that general baseline knowledge about hospitals and how they care for children when they are unwell, as previously discussed. By their nature, of involving a number of children simultaneously, they tend not to contain information that is relevant to specific medical procedures or treatment, although there is sometimes the opportunity for children and their parents to speak individually with a doctor, nurse or play specialist and to raise any specific concerns or questions they may have. Generally speaking though, pre-admission 'clubs' of this nature are concerned with preparing children for their admission to hospital first and foremost and less with anything that may happen to them thereafter.

Lansdown (1996), in referring to a study by Glasper et al. (1992), suggests that when compared to children who received no organized preparation, those who had attended a pre-admission programme of the type outlined above did benefit from the opportunity to learn about admission to hospital. The study did highlight, however, that pre-admission programmes of this nature were relatively poorly attended, which perhaps calls into question both their overall and their cost effectiveness.

Work in schools

One way that some play specialists have developed their provision in this area is to deliver a programme of preparation to groups of pre-school and primary school-aged children within school settings. This type of preparation programme is currently being run in a number of areas around the UK, one of which is profiled by Fairburn in *Hospital Play: Snapshots of Good Practice* (Maras 2003). In the example given, the need for a preparation project based in schools – a 'Hospital Awareness Scheme' – was identified after the attendance at the pre-admission 'Saturday Club' reached a very low level. The play specialists involved in this work recognized that there was a need to change their methods of preparation to ensure that as many children as possible benefited. Their aim therefore was to go to groups of children, meeting with them in a familiar and non-threatening environment, and to introduce them to situations commonly faced on admission to hospital. In the event of this happening at some stage, the theory is that those children in receipt of such sessions will have at least received a baseline level of preparation and therefore will, it is hoped, cope better as a result.

Specific preparation

The what, why, who, where, when (phew!) and how approach

The guidance for children's professionals in both the UN Convention on the Rights of the Child (1990) and the Children Act (1989) outlines clearly its advocacy for the inclusion of children in important decisions affecting their lives. Also clear in these two documents is an assertion that such opportunities to be included in these decisions can only be given to children if they are offered information and support by various means and appropriate to their age and cognitive ability. Preparation through play gives a good example of the aims of this guidance.

Lansdown (1996) stresses the importance of discussing with children in hospital, or due to be admitted to hospital, not only what is going to happen, but also why and how those events will take place. It is his observation that it is simply not enough to tell children what is going to happen and that this information almost invariably also requires an adequate explanation of why a certain procedure or treatment is to go ahead. It is widely acknowledged by healthcare professionals in various settings that sick children are often acutely aware if they are not receiving adequate or accurate information about their condition or its treatment.

This sense of not being kept in the picture can also become highly distressing for children in this situation. In recognition of this, play specialists aim, where at all possible, to explain as much as is deemed to be appropriate to the children in their care. Due consideration given to the cognitive ability and experiences of individual children influences the content of the information given about their condition, treatment and the care they should expect to receive. This therefore accounts for why preparation for procedures and information sharing with children about conditions or treatment regimens constitutes quite a sizeable chunk of the role of play specialists working in a variety of healthcare settings.

In the audit and quality-assessment tool *Play for Health*, Walker (2006) states that 'research has demonstrated that preparation through play reduces anxiety, supports effective pain management and encourages co-operative behaviour' (p.23) and in doing so, offers a succinct but effective rationale behind why preparation through play must be offered to sick children. Herein lies an important distinction, also, for all those involved in helping to prepare children for strange, difficult or unpleasant medical procedures, play specialists included: it is not merely enough to present children with a whole heap of information, be it verbal or written, and to hope they will adequately understand or assimilate it independently to then be adequately enabled to cope with the procedure when it happens. The key to the vast majority of the preparation work undertaken by play specialists is that it incorporates elements of play and uses illustrative material with the aim of enabling children to take on new or troubling information at a much deeper level of understanding than merely telling them what is going to happen to them.

It is important to recognize the distinction that can be made between play as a central feature in the preparation activities specifically offered by play specialists and verbal explanations offered to children by many other adults, from parents to doctors. An example of this distinction is seen in a description of six-year-old Harry, given by Harvey and Hales-Tooke (1972), who is told about his forthcoming operation by both a nurse and the play specialist. They illustrate the ways in which play can be more effective in the consolidation of information than an explanation in just words alone by describing how Harry was told by the nurse that he would be given an injection that would make him very sleepy and that he would not feel any pain when the operation took place. He was also told that for several days after his eye operation he would need to wear a cotton pad over his eye to prevent him from using that eye while it healed. At this point in the preparation the playleader [sic.] demonstrated for Harry what this meant and would look like on a teddy bear, and then allowed him to experiment through play, putting the pad on the playleader's eye, and eventually trying it on his own eye and asking for a mirror so that he could see how it looked.

While the verbal explanation offered to Harry by the nurse was accurate, given sensitively and appropriately for his age and level of understanding, the position of Harvey and Hales-Tooke is that a verbal explanation such as this is not enough on its own. It is their observation that the key element to the success of this example of preparation is that the child was able to engage in repetitive play and by doing so was able to gain a firmer grasp of what was going to happen and how he would be affected.

In this environment children may feel very out of control, not only of their ill bodies but also regarding a lot of the decisions that are made and by which they are affected. Through the introduction of aspects of mastery and control in preparation sessions, children can be helped to explore these feelings while also being able to regain a sense of control in the sense of safety found in play. By the use of a doll from which blood can be taken, for example, the play specialist is able to explain what venepuncture involves, honestly and in an appropriate amount of detail. Children not only see very clearly what such a procedure is like, but they can also be encouraged to handle the actual equipment that will in turn be used on them. They can have a go at experimenting with taking on the active role of 'doctor' or 'nurse' rather than being forced to adopt the more passive role of patient. They can also safely express – through a non-threatening third party of a doll or made up character – fears and emotional responses before the actual procedure takes place. By the observation of a child's responses within a preparation session, the play specialist can give more information or reassurance as appropriate and can also plan effectively how best to emotionally support a child through the procedure or treatment to follow in the most effective ways.

Specific and guided preparation through play offered by play specialists can be seen to be just that: specific and guided. It is 'specific' because it deals only with the procedure, condition or treatment that calls for information to be shared with the child. It is also 'specific' because it assumes that the child has the broad general knowledge of hospitals discussed in the previous section and does not need to repeat this information to be useful. Specific preparation therefore bypasses this foundation stage and moves to individual children's immediate needs, dictated by their current situation, and aims to increase their knowledge, thus enabling them to cope well enough to complete the necessary next stage in their diagnosis or treatment. There is also often a need to put the child's current situation into a context, bearing in mind his or her age and level of cognitive ability. This way, by understanding how our bodies usually work, for example, children can be helped to see why there is a concern that theirs is not working effectively and therefore why there is the need for further investigation or treatment.

This type of preparation is also seen as being 'guided' because it is distinct from normalizing free play, involving a fairly prescriptive approach by the play specialist, using particular resources or activities and aiming explicitly to increase a child's awareness of his or her illness, condition, treatment and any procedures he or she is facing. In contrast to the desirable outcomes of much more general preparation (what, why and who), through this specific, guided approach to information sharing with children, play specialists will attempt to establish the following:

- *How* do/should bodies function effectively?

- *Why* am I ill? (Possible causes include bacteria, viruses, genetic factors, etc.)

- *What* has happened to cause my body to not work so effectively?

- *How* are we going to find out what is happening? (By looking at a sample of your blood/urine/skin; by looking further inside your body)

- *What* treatment/procedure do I need? (Blood test; urine test; scan; IV infusion, etc.)

- *Why* do I need this? (To look for 'X'; to decide on the best treatment)

- *Who* will do this? (The doctor/nurse/phlebotomist)

- *Where* will it be done? (In the treatment room/in your room/by your bed)

- *How* will it happen? (A small amount of blood will be taken from a vein using a very fine needle/you will do a wee in a small sample bottle, which will then be tested/a very fine plastic tube will be put into a vein and your liquid medicine will be put into your body through it; etc.).

In some cases, more often with older children and adolescents, depending upon the understanding or concerns of the individuals involved, preparation may include some discussion or activities that also broach the following areas:

- *What if* the procedure does not go ahead?

- *What if* the procedure/treatment is not effective?

- *What next?* Will there be more treatment/investigations in the future?

Clearly the preparation offered to children by play specialists can involve an enormous amount of information that can be complex and difficult to understand or that requires a lot of emotional and psychological energy to take on board, particularly taking into account that being ill may already be quite a stressful business. Play specialists are, by and large, highly diligent in sourcing precise information so that any preparation offered is accurate and reliable for each individual child with whom they work. Therefore the large body of information that is outlined above is quite likely to be given to children in a number of manageable chunks – depending on the urgency of the situation – or will be simplified to a manageable quantity for them according to their immediate needs, age and level of understanding. Some information may also be given post-procedurally, an area of information sharing that will be discussed in more detail later.

Some of the most common procedures and situations about which play specialists aim to share information with children and young people will include:

- venepuncture, more commonly referred to as 'blood tests'

- general anaesthetic, using gas or intravenous medication

- surgery: 'having an operation'

- scans, such as X-rays, MRI, CT, ultrasound and possibly radioisotope scans

- allergy testing, such as food challenges or 'skin prick' testing

- intravenous lines, such as cannulae, Hickman lines or portocaths

- feeding tubes, such as PEG or nasogastric feeding

- radiotherapy treatment, including casting a facial jig

- discussion about specific conditions, such as diabetes, leukaemia, asthma or eczema.

Play specialists will try to offer a package of preparation for children facing any situation that arises while they are receiving treatment, having been informed of the child's situation by another member of the multidisciplinary team, and having gathered all the necessary information and resources necessary to give sound, reliable information to the child. However there is a range of procedures or scenarios that constitute the most common types of referral for preparation through play. Most play teams will have a bank of resources that are ready for use in response to such referrals although what these collected resources contain clearly depends on a number of different factors, including whether any specialist care is carried out in a particular ward or the openness of the wider team to the value of preparation through play.

Obstructions to good preparation

When preparation through play is planned and delivered well, there is no denying the positive effect it can have on a child's experience of his or her illness, treatment or hospitalization. However, in spite of a wealth of anecdotal and research-based evidence showing its effectiveness in helping children cope with a range of strange and sometimes distressing experiences, there are a number of factors that commonly obstruct or can threaten to undermine the effectiveness of the preparation that play specialists offer to children in their care.

Unwillingness of multidisciplinary teams to refer patients or to recognize the merits of preparation through play

Despite the fact that on a general level, recognition of the therapeutic benefits of play for sick children has been gradually growing over the past half-century or more, at a more local level play specialists often still have to battle to get their voice heard and the value of their work recognized within multidisciplinary teams. Some of this difficulty is caused by the issues largely outlined in Chapter 2 of this book. These include the fact that play specialists are yet to be recognized officially as allied health professionals, that there are many misconceptions around play and the specific function or benefit of play for sick children and also that the job title of play specialists can be ambiguous and unhelpful in communicating the scope and value of the role. In addition to this is the fact that multidisciplinary teams are continually changing, losing and gaining staff on a very regular basis, their dynamics and general ethos changing subtly with each change.

The implication for play specialists in the face of all this is that there will inevitably be times when the multidisciplinary team is more receptive and embracing of their work and therefore more likely to use them to good effect and recognize them as a strong, influential and valuable team player. There equally will be periods of time where play is deemed to be of less importance, the play specialists' role is less widely understood or appreciated and as a result during these periods play specialists will need to work harder to gain the recognition they and their work deserves. Similarly, when a play specialist is a newly appointed member of staff, it may take quite some time for his or her ability to work effectively with children and young people to be recognized and to make a difference to the work of the wider multidisciplinary team.

At these times, the unwillingness of the multidisciplinary team to recognize the value of play services for sick children may well lead to a certain unwillingness by colleagues to refer patients to the play specialist for preparation or emotional support, such as that provided by good distraction during procedures. It may also take a considerable amount of time for colleagues automatically to think to ask the play specialist to be more involved with patients and families as required. This in itself can be seen to be a barrier to effective work, requiring a patient and persistent response by play specialists who are prepared to show the merits of their work practically and consistently educate and re-educate the ever-changing multidisciplinary team on the benefits of good quality play provision for sick children.

Lack of time, resources or information

If any preparation offered for procedures is going to be effective and meaningful for sick children, their parents and sometimes their siblings, it needs to be supported by adequate time, high quality useful resources and reliable information. It is not an uncommon occurrence for the involvement of the play specialists to be requested after a procedure has begun, where there has been little or no preparation offered and where a child has already become fearful or distressed. This is clearly far from ideal as it allows the play specialist little or no time to gather the necessary information about the child's treatment or procedure, to talk to the child in a meaningful, non-pressurized manner and to bring a selection of useful preparation resources. Because of this, the likelihood of the procedure being completed successfully is diminished and the likelihood of the child experiencing distress and confusion is significantly increased.

Ideally the play specialist should be informed of a child's need for treatment or an invasive intervention at the earliest possible point so that he or she can start to plan the preparation session that will be best suited and most useful for that child.

Panic, stress or urgency

Since an overarching aim of preparation is the reduction of anxiety or worry, it is logical then that a child's feelings of fear, panic and distress present a major obstacle to its effectiveness. This obstacle is further increased if undue pressure is placed on play specialists who are expected to deliver useful and effective preparation either where there is insufficient time or where it has not been considered to be a priority.

As discussed above, play specialists are often called to assist with a procedure either immediately before it is due to start or even once it is already under way. The need to appease the child and to allow the procedure to progress successfully takes on a particular urgency at a point when time is often not in abundance. Clearly this is not an ideal situation for the play specialist, who is somehow expected to calm the child, quickly explain what is happening and then by some means make him or her cope with what is happening. Nor is it at all ideal for the child him- or herself, who is likely to experience feelings of enormous stress, especially when having no control over what is happening to him or her. If the play specialist is asked at just such a point to explain to a child what is happening and why, there is a great likelihood that his or her work will be significantly less useful to the child, since it is much harder to hear, process and make sense of important information if the child's level of anxiety is already raised (Lansdown 1996).

Lack of parental consent

Play specialists aim always to impart information to children that is reliable and honest. However, they are bound by the wishes of a child's parents who may state that they do not wish their child to be told certain facts or – in extreme cases – may not want their child to be told anything about what is going to happen to him or her in hospital or in the course of his or her treatment. Parental anxiety is known to be an important factor contributing to whether preparation is as effective as possible (Lansdown 1996). However, it is also worth considering the extent to which obstructive behaviour with regard to a child receiving information about his or her condition or its treatment may largely be an expression of the parents' fears and worries. It may also be a reflection of the general communication style of a family where, for example, there may be little or no discussion around other challenging, embarrassing or difficult areas including sex or emotions.

Where there is a lack of parental consent over their children receiving important information, the play specialist is in the difficult position of knowing the benefits that such discussion could have for the child, while really having no choice but to respect his or her parents' wishes. With the support of colleagues from the wider multi-disciplinary team, it may be possible for the play specialist to broach the subject of information sharing with parents who are hesitant or obstructive and for some agreement to be reached over boundary setting and the content of any preparation that is offered to children in this situation.

Is imparting information honestly always the best policy?

In spite of all the facts that children may be told during preparation sessions, one of the biggest concerns that they consistently have is whether the procedure or treatment they are facing will be a painful or unpleasant experience. This further highlights the important way in which information sharing with sick children and emotionally supporting them are interlinked. While children can often be helped to cope with medical interventions by being appropriately informed and helped to understand what is happening to them, they frequently ask questions that are direct and can be difficult to answer but which require a fine balance of honesty and sensitivity in any answers.

The drive of adults as carers and parents is to protect the children in their care and not purposefully or deliberately to expose them to difficult or horrible experiences. To knowingly put a child through a procedure that is going to be painful or unpleasant goes against all of those good intentions to prevent him or her being exposed to stress or trauma, and yet parents and professionals alike, when involved in caring for sick children, have to do this on a very regular basis. For healthcare professionals, including play specialists, understanding how and why this presents a moral and emotional challenge is important when considering how to talk with children about painful or distressing experiences.

Parents may prefer to avoid discussing frightening subjects or issues such as pain with children because they are concerned about upsetting them or causing them more distress. This desire to avoid difficult subjects may mean that parents, on the one hand, may opt to rely on members of staff, including the play specialist, to provide any explanation to their child, instead of trying to keep the lines of communication open themselves. In doing so, they may inadvertently give their child the impression that expressing strong emotions is somehow taboo or wrong. Alternatively, parents may either tell their child that a procedure will not be painful or challenging even if it is known to be unpleasant or, in a more extreme scenario, they may refuse to give consent for their child to be told anything about an upcoming procedure, thinking that this will prevent their child experiencing any undue worry or upset. None of these approaches is ideal, although the former is more desirable than the latter, since this way at least the child is told about what a procedure involves. The most desirable approach is one where parents and the other adults involved in a child's care are united in both the level of information that a child is offered and the methods of preparation that are used to aid a child's understanding of his or her situation.

In considering the play specialist's approach, there is always a concern that by giving children details about a procedure that is potentially distressing and contains the likelihood of having to endure pain or discomfort, the child will refuse to comply with those involved in that procedure or treatment. The play specialist needs always to be mindful of the possibility of giving a child too much information, which causes him or her to feel more anxious rather than being a reassurance. Recognition of the need to strike a good balance between preparing children by given them appropriately pitched information without allowing them to feel overwhelmed is the key to handling this sensitive area.

The challenge to address children's concerns over pain, discomfort or fear highlights the importance for play specialists to have developed a relationship of trust with their patients. Even if this relationship needs to be established within a very short space of time or is allowed to develop over a longer period, it is one that allows for the discussion of difficult subjects. To the children they work with, play specialists are reliable and supportive people, whom they trust to answer their questions as fully and as honestly as possible. Play specialists tell and show them what will happen during a procedure, help them to understand why it must happen, how it will happen and, where necessary or appropriate, tell them honestly what that experience will be like.

Information sharing with sick children and young people is a mainstay of the play specialist's work. Armed with adequate information that is pitched appropriately according to their age and cognitive ability, children can be helped to cope with the situations they may face in the course of being ill, in hospital and throughout their recovery. If that information is denied them by circumstance or by a misguided desire to 'protect' them from stress or worry, they may be placed in danger of struggling unnecessarily with their situation. Children trust play specialists to give them real, accurate information, to help them to cope with the experiences they must go through and to find out what those experiences are like for them. This aspect of the play specialist's role is outlined in Figure 6.1. Furthermore, it could be suggested that the play specialist's approach to preparing children for painful or unpleasant procedures contains the following four key elements:

- *Honest description*: verbal explanation with practical demonstration.

- *Reassurance of support*: play specialist's role during procedures is outlined.

- *Plan for the moment*: 'patient role' is outlined plus the distraction activities that are available.

- *Review the situation*: post-procedural discussion/play.

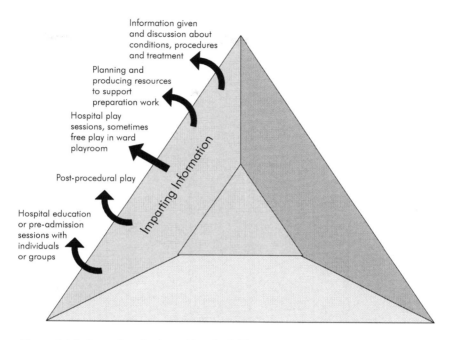

Figure 6.1 Information sharing with sick children

In Conclusion...

All children staying in hospital should have daily access to a play specialist. [Furthermore] the use of play techniques should be used across the multidisciplinary team caring for children...with play specialists taking a lead in modelling techniques that other staff can then adopt. (Department of Health 2003, p.14)

Throughout the course of this book, a model has gradually been pieced together that aims to outline in some detail the three main aspects of the play specialist's role in working with sick children and young people. Until this point these aspects – normalizing play, emotional support and imparting information – have largely been seen and described only as three separate parts of the role. In Figure 7.1, these parts are brought together and the role presented in its fullness and therefore it is put forward that this model represents an ideal method of providing play services for all children who are unwell and may be in hospital, whose individual needs have been assessed, and where there are relatively clear goals or outcomes to be reached, even if these include merely for the child to have fun, to be allowed to play freely or to socialize with children of a similar age, for example.

This model aims to demonstrate that while each aspect is given equal priority and is understood to be important and significant in

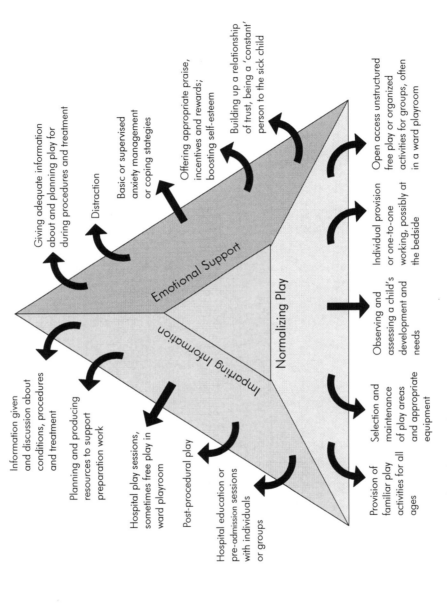

Figure 7.1 The threefold role of the play specialist

Information given
and discussion about
conditions, procedures
and treatment

Planning and producing
resources to support
preparation work

Hospital play sessions,
sometimes free play in
ward playroom

Post-procedural play

Hospital education or
pre-admission sessions
with individuals
or groups

Giving adequate information
about and planning play for
during procedures and treatment

Distraction

Basic or supervised
anxiety management
or coping stategies

Offering appropriate praise,
incentives and rewards;
boosting self-esteem

Building up a relationship
of trust, being a 'constant'
person to the sick child

Emotional Support

Imparting Information

Normalizing Play

Provision of
familiar play
activities for all
ages

Selection and
maintenance
of play areas
and appropriate
equipment

Observing and
assessing a child's
development and
needs

Individual provision
or one-to-one
working, possibly at
the bedside

Open access unstructured
free play or organized
activities for groups, often
in a ward playroom

the experiences of children who are ill, and who are being made well, when all the three aspects of play for these sick children are delivered they complement and support each other and in doing so aid the child's ability to cope as well and as effectively as possible with the situation he or she faces.

In this vein, then, there is a central section to the model still to be accounted for, that until this point has remained blank. This central point, featured in detail in Figure 7.2, represents the crossover point of the three separate aspects of the work undertaken and carried out by play specialists engaged in providing play services to sick children and their families. It is within this centre point that the optimal outcome of the play specialist's work is presented. Here, not only are the three separate aspects of the role brought together, but it is clearly demonstrated that they can significantly influence and complement each other in the play specialist's work in aiming to respond effectively to the needs and within the experiences of sick children. While reaching this interrelation of the three aspects of the role should be something of an aim for the play specialist in his or her work with individual children, it must be realized that what this model presents is the ideal, of course, and not necessarily the reality. It is therefore clear that in some cases it simply is not possible to deliver play provision equally across all three aspects.

The child brought to hospital in an emergency situation, for example, may not be able to receive much – if any – preparation for what his or her initial treatment may involve and may therefore experience sensations or strong emotional responses caused by procedures without receiving much in the way of an explanation. Similarly, in many clinical settings it is still the case that invasive procedures regularly begin without other members of the wider multidisciplinary team thinking or choosing to involve the play specialist. Therefore nothing is done either to prepare children or support them in coping with any pain or distress they may experience. Sometimes, in such situations, it is only once the procedure has already begun that the

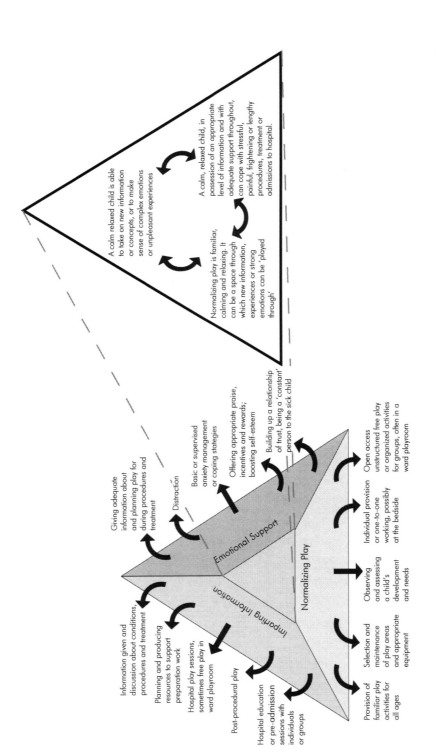

Figure 7.2 The interconnectedness of the three central aspects of the role of the play specialist — and the optimal outcome of the play specialist's work with sick children

assistance of the play specialist, to support a child who has become significantly distressed, is called upon.

There may equally be times when even normalizing play is not provided to an adequate level or in an accessible way for all children to whom it could be beneficial. Many waiting areas in a variety of healthcare settings, particularly in adult-orientated environments, are inadequately equipped for paediatric patients, for example. Furthermore, on hospital wards there is still the risk of observing a child to be 'the good child', who is quiet and relatively undemanding and who therefore appears to be coping. Such patients were first identified as a concern by the Robertsons in the 1950s since, by their unassuming nature, these children may not be perceived to be a priority or particularly in need. All the while, however, these could be children who would benefit significantly from the opportunity to play freely, or whose quiet demeanour covers an underlying anxiety that could be addressed or played through during free play sessions.

All these scenarios and more can affect the likelihood of sick children receiving the most desirable play provision when they need it, and yet it is still important as professionals to have an ideal as a goal to work towards. Professional practice that has a clear and ultimately achievable goal to aim towards serves to ensure that all children – whatever and wherever the healthcare setting – have adequate opportunities to play, with access to safe, stimulating play facilities, and an informed, appropriate, supportive and often therapeutic response made to their individual needs while they are in receipt of the care of the multidisciplinary team as a whole and particularly that of the play specialist.

References

Alderson, P. (1990) *Choosing for Children: Parents' Consent to Surgery.* Oxford: Oxford University Press.

Aynsley-Green, A. (2005) 'Great Ormond Street welcomes drive to improve pain relief.' Great Ormond Street Press Release, October. Accessed on 16 November 2008 at: www.ich.ucl.ac.uk/pressoffice/pressrelease_00380.

Azarnoff, P. (ed.) (1986) *Medically-Oriented Play for Children in Health Care: The Issues.* Santa Monica, CA: Pediatric Projects.

Barnardo's and Transport 2000 Association of London Government (2004) *Stop Look and Listen: Children Talk about Traffic.* Essex: Barnardo's.

Barrell, S. (2004, 2nd Edition) *Brothers and Sisters.* Witney, Oxon: Sarah Barrell.

Batmanghelidjh, C. (2006) *Shattered Lives: Children who Live with Courage and Dignity.* London: Jessica Kingsley Publishers.

Belson, P. (1987) 'A plea for play.' *Nursing Times 83,* 26, 16–18.

Bibace, R. and Walsh, M.E. (1981) 'Children's conceptions of illness.' *New Directions for Child Development 14.*

Bluebond-Langner, M. (1978) *The Private Worlds of Dying Children.* Chichester: Princeton University Press.

Bristol City Council (2009) 'Hospital Education Service.' Children's and Young People's Services website. Accessed on January 10 at: www.bristol-cyps.org.uk/services/cyp/he_service.html.

Brown, F. (ed.) (2003) *Playwork: Theory and Practice.* Buckingham: Open University Press.

Cattanach, A. (2003) *Introduction to Play Therapy.* Hove: Brunner-Routledge.

Clements, R. (1998) *Wanted: Strong Children with Healthy Imaginations.* Hempstead, NY: Playground Environments.

Clements, R. (2004) 'An investigation of the status of outdoor play.' *Contemporary Issues in Early Childhood 5,* 1, 68–80.

Collins English Dictionary: Millennium Edition (1999) Glasgow: HarperCollins.

Cook, P. (1999) *Supporting Sick Children and their Families.* London: Bailliére Tindall.

Dartford and Gravesham NHS Trust (2007) *Guidelines for Holding Children During Clinical Procedures.* Kent: D&GNHS Trust.

Dempsey, S. (2008) *Extreme Parenting: Parenting your Child with a Chronic Illness.* London: Jessica Kingsley Publishers.

Department of Health (2003) *National Service Framework for Children and Young People and Maternity Services: Standard for Hospital Services.* London: Department of Health.

Duffy, B. (2007) *All About...Messy Play.* London: Early Years Foundation Stage.

Dunn, J. (1988) *The Beginnings of Social Understanding.* Oxford: Blackwell.

Eiser, C. (1990) *Chronic Childhood Disease: An Introduction to Psychological Theory and Research.* Cambridge: Cambridge University Press.

Eiser, C. (1995, 2nd Edition) *Growing up with a Chronic Disease.* London: Jessica Kingsley Publishers.

Eliot, L. (1999) *Early Intelligence: How the Brain and Mind Develop in the First Five Years of Life.* London: Penguin.

Fawcett, M. (1996) *Learning Through Child Observation.* London: Jessica Kingsley Publishers.

Gaffney, A. and Dunne, E.A. (1987) 'Children's understanding of the causality of pain.' *Pain 29*, 91–104.

Gaynard, D., Wolfer, J., Goldberger, J., Thompson, R., Redburn, L. and Laidly, L. (1990) *Psychosocial Care of Children in Hospitals: A Clinical Practice Manual from the ACCH Child Life Research Project.* Washington, DC: Association for the Care of Children's Health (ACCH).

Gerhardt, S. (2004) *Why Love Matters.* Hove: Routledge.

Goldman, A. (ed.) (1998) *Care of the Dying Child.* Oxford: Oxford University Press.

Goldschmeid, E. and Jackson, S. (2004, 2nd Edition) *People Under Three: Young Children in Day Care.* Abingdon: Routledge.

Gopnik, A., Meltzoff, A. and Kuhl, P. (1999) *How Babies Think.* London: Weidenfield and Nicolson.

Hales-Tooke, A. (1973) *Children in Hospital: The Parents' View.* London: Priory Press.

Harvey, S. and Hales-Tooke, A. (eds) (1972) *Play in Hospital.* London: Faber Health Service Journal.

Hendrick, H. (1997) *Children, Childhood and English Society 1880–1990.* Cambridge: Cambridge University Press.

Hoffman, A.D., Becker, R.D. and Gabriel, H.P. (1976) *The Hospitalized Adolescent.* New York, NY: The Free Press.

Hogg, C. (1990) *Quality Management for Children: Play in Hospital.* London: Hospital Liaison Committee.

Hubbuck, C. (2003) 'Treatment of children with severe burns.' *The Lancet Extreme Medicine 362*, December, S44–S45.

Hughes, B. (1984) 'Play: a definition by synthesis.' In *Play Provision and Play Needs.* Lancaster: PlayEducation.

Hughes, B. (1996) *A Playworker's Taxonomy of Play Types.* London: PLAYLINK.

Hughes, B. (2001) *Evolutionary Playwork and Reflective Analytic Practice.* London: Routledge.

James, A. and Prout, A. (eds) (1997) *Constructing and Reconstructing Childhood: Contemporary Issues in the Sociological Study of Childhood.* London: Falmer Press.

Jenks, C. (1996) *Key Ideas: Childhood.* London: Routledge.

Jolly, H. (1976) 'Why children must be able to play in hospital.' *The Times*, 21 April.

Jolly, J. (1981) *The Other Side of Paediatrics*. London: Macmillan Press.

Kennedy, I. (2001) *Learning from Bristol: The report of the public inquiry into children's heart surgery at the Bristol Royal Infirmary 1984–1995*. Crown copyright.

Laming, Lord (2003) *The Victoria Climbié Inquiry*. Crown Copyright.

Lansdown, R. (1980) *More than Sympathy*. London: Tavistock Publications.

Lansdown, R. (1996) *Children in Hospital: A Guide for Family and Carers*. Oxford: Oxford University Press.

Lansdown, R. and Sokel, B. (1993) 'Commissioned review: approaches to pain management in children.' *ACPP Review and Newsletter 15*, 3, 105–111.

Lansdown, R. and Walker, M. (1996) *Your Child's Development from Birth to Adolescence*. London: Frances Lincoln Limited.

Laurent, C. (2008) 'Adolescent services: smells like teen spirit.' *Health Service Journal, 01 September.* Accessed on 2 October 2008 at: www.hsj.co.uk/adolescent-services-smells-like-teen-spirit/1796181.article.

Lindon, J. (2001) *Understanding Children's Play*. Cheltenham: Nelson Thornes.

Manning-Morton, J. and Thorp, M. (2003) *Key Times for Play: The First Three Years*. Maidenhead: Open University Press.

Maras, P. (ed.) (2003) *Hospital Play: Snapshots of Good Practice*. London: Hospital Play Staff Education Trust (HPSET).

Marks, D.E., Murray, M., Evans, B. and Willig, C. (2000) *Health Psychology: Theory, Research and Practice*. London: Sage.

Meadows, S. (1986) *Understanding Child Development*. London: Routledge.

Meadows, S. (1993) *The Child as Thinker: The Development and Acquisition of Cognition in Childhood*. London: Routledge.

National Association of Hospital Play Specialists (NAHPS) (2002) *Guidelines for Professional Practice: 5 – Play Preparation*. London: NAHPS.

National Association for the Welfare of Children in Hospital (NAWCH) (1990) *Setting Standards for Adolescents in Hospital*. London: NAWCH.

National Statistics (2004) 'Mortality statistics: Childhood, infant and perinatal.' Accessed on 12 September 2008 at: www.statistics.gov.uk/downloads/theme_health/DH3_2002/DH3_35.pdf.

Pica, R. (2003) *Your Active Child: How to Boost Physical, Emotional and Cognitive Development Through Age-appropriate Activity*. Chicago, IL: Contemporary Books.

Platt, H. (1959) *The Welfare of Children in Hospital*. London: HMSO.

Robertson, J. (1970, 2nd Edition) *Young Children in Hospital*. London: Tavistock Press.

Rutter, M. (1972) *Maternal Deprivation Reassessed*. Harmondsworth: Penguin.

Ryan, T. and Walker, R. (2003, 2nd (revised) Edition) *Life Story Work: A Practical Guide to Helping Children Understand their Past*. London: British Association for Adoption and Fostering (BAAF).

Save the Children (1989) *Hospital: A Deprived Environment for Children? The Case for Hospital Play Schemes*. London: Save the Children.

Savory, J. and Bennett, M. (2006) 'Managing children's pain.' *Nursing Times 102*, 9, 57–61.

Sheridan, M. (1977) *Spontaneous Play in Early Childhood from Birth to Six Years.* Windsor: NFER-Nelson Publishing.

Smith, P.K., Cowie, H. and Blades, M. (2003, 4th Edition) *Understanding Children's Development.* Oxford: Wiley Blackwell.

Sutton-Smith, B. (1997) *The Ambiguity of Play.* Cambridge, MA: Harvard University Press.

Thorp, S. (2006) 'The power of play.' *Children Now,* 30 August–5 September, 20–21.

United Nations Convention on the Rights of the Child 1990.

Walker, J. (2006) *Play for Health: Delivering and Auditing Quality in Hospital Play Services.* London: National Association of Hospital Play Staff (NAHPS).

Weiss, L. (1987) 'Preparation for surgery and unpleasant procedures.' *NAHPS Let's Play No 7.*

Weller, B. (1980) *Helping Sick Children Play.* London: Baillière Tindall.

Yerrell, S. (1998) 'Sensory stimulation with neonates.' *The Journal of the National Association of Hospital Play Staff,* Summer, 7–9.

Young, C. (2007) *Entertaining and Educating Babies and Toddlers.* London: Usborne.

Young, C. (2008) *Entertaining and Educating Young Children.* London: Usborne.

Websites consulted and cited

Bristol City Council:

www.bristol-cyps.org.uk

British Association of Play Therapists:

www.bapt.info

Children's Services Mapping:

www.childrensmapping.org.uk

Hospital Play Specialists Association of Aotearoa/New Zealand Inc:

www.hospitalplay.org.nz

Hospital Play Staff Education Trust:

www.hpset.org.uk

National Association of Hospital Play Staff:

www.nahps.org.uk

NHS Careers:

www.nhscareers.nhs.uk

University of Akron, Ohio, Child Life:

www.uakron.edu/colleges/faa/schools/fcs/childlife/Action for Sick Children 25–6, 32

Subject Index

Armstrong, George 16
art and craft activities 133–4

babies
  cognitive development in
    90–3
  effects of hospital on
    development 67–9,
    79
  eye contact with 78
  needs of in hospital 75–9
  play needs of 71–5
  and the play specialist
    69–71, 72–5, 76,
    79–80
  stimulation for 78
  support for parents
    75–6
  talking to 77–8
  touching and holding 77
  uses of senses 79
  view of development
    70–1
Bristol Royal Infirmary 29
British Association of Play
  Therapists (BAPT) 40
broad pre-procedure
  preparation 237–42
Brook Hospital, Woolwich
  25

Central Health Services
  Council 23

children
  evacuation of during the
    Second World War
    18–19
  and the NSF 29–30
  nineteenth century
    attitudes to 17
  'normal' and 'abnormal'
    development 64–5,
    122–4
  mortality rates among
    180–1
  perception of play 127–9
  in residential care 20
  stress caused by
    separation 16, 19,
    20–3, 82–3
  see also babies; middle
    childhood;
    teenagers; young
    children
Children Act (1948) 19
Children in Hospital
  (Lansdown) 15–16
children's development in
  hospital 125–6
  and babies 67–9
  and importance of play
    126–7, 159
children's experience of
  hospital
  and acute illness 175–8

admission to hospital
  175–8
and babies 67–9, 79
and chronic illness
  178–80
communicating needs
  172–4, 217–55
consultation with 194–6
and emotional needs
  158–9, 164–5, 196,
  214–15
impact of on normal child
  development 6
and invasive medical
  procedures 191–2,
  209–11
and James and Joyce
  Robertson 21–3,
  32, 125
loss of bodily control
  192–3
and middle childhood
  86–8
and the NAWCH 25–6
number of staff seeing
  children 169–71
and observation of other
  patients 167–9
and pain 187–90
and physical restraint
  209–11
and the Platt Report
  23–4, 125

Author Index

Printed in Great Britain
by Amazon

29906901R00152